LATE YOU

Praise for *Late Youth*

———————

'Seventy-four celebrities, all wrinkly and proud of it, give their view of what life is like once you've passed the 50-year milestone. The mood is upbeat and often tongue-in-cheek as the authors write about the things that keep them young . . . a wonderfully reassuring charity book'
– *The Good Book Guide*

'An absolutely delightful miscellany – always good to shoot a paean for age and from such distinguished guns, too'
– Mavis Cheek

'Excellent . . . what a beautifully produced book!'
– Martyn Goff

LATE YOUTH

AN ANTHOLOGY
CELEBRATING THE JOYS
OF BEING OVER FIFTY

Edited with an Introduction by Susanna Johnston

ARCADIA BOOKS

Arcadia Books Ltd
15-16 Nassau Street
London W1W 7AB

www.arcadiabooks.co.uk

First hardback edition published in the UK 2005
Reprinted October 2005
First paperback edition published November 2006
Foreword © Carole Blake 2005
Introduction © Susanna Johnston 2005
Individual copyright rests with each author

A catalogue record for this book is available from the British Library.

ISBN 1-905147-09-0

Typeset in Garamond by Basement Press, London
Printed in Finland by WS Bookwell

Arcadia Books distributors are as follows:

in the UK and elsewhere in Europe:
Turnaround Publishers Services
Unit 3, Olympia Trading Estate
Coburg Road
London N22 6TZ

in the USA and Canada:
Independent Publishers Group
814 N. Franklin St.
Chicago, IL 60610

in Australia:
Tower Books
PO Box 213
Brookvale, NSW 2100

in New Zealand:
Addenda
Box 78224
Grey Lynn
Auckland

in South Africa:
Quartet Sales and Marketing
PO Box 1218
Northcliffe
Johannesburg 2115

Arcadia Books is the *Sunday Times* Small Publisher of the Year

To Bertram Weatherall. My first grandchild. Aged sixteen.

ACKNOWLEDGEMENTS

'There Are Advantages' by Maureen Cleave was adapted from the article 'Ancient and Modern', which first appeared in the *Telegraph Magazine* 17 February 2000.

'"Sexagenarian" Is Such A Beautiful Word – It Comes After "Sex" In The Dictionary' by Jilly Cooper was adapted from an article that first appeared in the *Weekend Mail* in February 1997.

'The Stage In Life' by Deborah Devonshire is taken from *Counting my Chickens*, published in 2001 by Long Barn Books.

'A Classic Slipstream Situation' by Elizabeth Jane Howard is from her book *Slipstream*, published in 2002 by Macmillan.

Excerpt from *The Time Diaries Of Julian Fane* is reproduced by kind permission of the Book Guild Ltd.

CONTENTS

Foreword

A BIG thank you to Arcadia for donating part of the profits from this book to the Book Trade Benevolent Society: the book trade charity. The BTBS and I are proud to be part of this inspirational volume, celebrating the joys of being over fifty.

The BTBS is actually even more mature than that; we're more than *one hundred and fifty* and proud of it. Proud of being the only welfare charity working within the British book trade – and perhaps in the world.

Publishing is a very sociable business, but it's one that now works within an unforgiving marketplace and a very harsh working environment. Companies large and small (publishers, booksellers, wholesalers, agencies) sometimes shed staff, and their pension schemes often fail to provide the expected cushion against redundancy. In a trade with a shrinking workforce, it can be daunting to try to restart a career. The BTBS can help in a number of ways.

We run a help-line to provide confidential information on any trade-related issue: redundancy, retraining, pensions shortfall. The Retreat in Kings Langley, Hertfordshire, provides subsidized housing in an attractive garden environment to people, mostly over fifty but not necessarily so, who want to live in a community of book-loving people.

We have a grants programme that can react quickly to urgent need, to carers or those with health or disability problems, as well as giving assistance with financial difficulties, essential travel costs, computers – even carpets and domestic equipment. We can provide one-off or regular grants and are very proud of the fact that we have never refused a legitimate request, whatever the state of our cash flow at the time.

We're proud to help so many people who might otherwise have nowhere else to turn, proud of running The Retreat and proud to be able to provide so many opportunities for people in publishing to fundraise in a way that is fun too.

I think we could a coin a word: 'funraise'. Take a look at our website to see pictures from 'The Walkies': our summer walk around London, which sees five or six hundred members of the book trade, many of them dressed on a theme taken from books or authors, lurch from bookshop to publishing house, sponsored for every step and drink on the way. It can be highly alarming for 'civilians' caught in the path of our charity walk!

We hold sales of donated books, we organize London Marathon places for people willing to raise sponsorship by running for us; we raise money from people who bet on the length of speeches at trade conferences. And a lot of people who should know better put on a cabaret every few years making fun of the book trade and its personalities. All the proceeds go to the BTBS, and those of us who have been in it spend a lot of time afterwards trying to live it down. No plan is too big or too silly if we think we can raise funds for the charity.

We receive very little regular financial support from the big corporations, so initiatives from projects like this are a real bonus.

Personally, I approve wholeheartedly of what this book celebrates. I'm very post-fifty, and my life took a definite upturn as I was reaching the big 'five-oh'. I haven't regretted a single moment since. Life as a grown-up is so much more fun than being young and anxious!

Carole Blake
Chairman of the Book Trade Benevolent Society

Introduction: Keep Running
Susanna Johnston

MOST of us have a deep-rooted fear of extinction, no matter what the circumstances or even how old we may be. A frail gentleman said not long ago: 'Nobody wants to live to be ninety – unless they're eighty-nine'. He then mentioned that he was eighty-nine.

I know one thing. I am not as old as I feel. I'm infinitely older. Through good fortune, escapism, mytho-mania or what you will, I am blessed with the assumption that everything is temporary. Wrinkles will vanish, stiffness will evaporate, and memory will return. All this discomfort and misery constitutes no more than a bad patch: to do with the weather, maybe. It could fit in with my mania for throwing things away prematurely. I'm crazy about it: three-quarter squeezed toothpaste tubes, half-empty date packets, slivers of soap, or what you will. It offers a chance for a fresh purchase and a new start – friskier than coming to the end of things. I have only recently discovered that I share this passion with many older people. My brother John tells me that he will merrily gulp down half a bottle of vodka in order to throw away the empty.

Although we are told that the over-fifties are neglected and ignored – particularly by advertising agencies – the topic of lost youth has always peppered pages. Booklets celebrating milestone birthdays sell like hotcakes in gift-shops: 'Now We Are Sixty', 'Midlife Crisis' and 'Never Too Late'. These products are jammed with chestnuts and dense with jokes about old age: 'A man is as young as the woman he feels' 'It doesn't matter unless you're a cheese' 'If the young only knew; if the old only could'.

Many references are made to Old Father William standing on his head, together with quips from Bette Davis: 'Old age is not for sissies.' The authors of these collections are hell-bent upon cheering us on our way. But do we really need to be cheered? Is it all that dreadful? Many over-fifties say that they enjoy things more than they used to and mind things less.

Some actually revel in being old. Sir Steven Runciman, the great Byzantine historian, claimed to have loved it. Perhaps he was helped by setting himself goals that were not always easy to achieve. He hoped, before he died, to have related romantically to at least one of those whose first names tallied with each letter in the alphabet. Even in his nineties he was thwarted by a missing letter. It is believed that it was the bearer of the letter 'Q' who gave him the slip.

Nigel Nicolson also proved himself to be a philosophical octogenarian. In 1997, on his eightieth birthday, he wrote for the *Sunday Telegraph*: 'If one hears less well, one can talk more; sleep less, read more; eat less, stay slim. Failing eyesight is restored by handsome spectacles; teeth by infinitely more convenient dentures; energy by idleness.'

Then there are those who loathe getting old, who either fight it tooth and nail or simply sit groaning. 'Fighting' often takes the form of a physical battle: maintenance and renewal of the body, physical jerks and facelifts. Groaning can be preferable to bright denial. Facelifts look quite marvellous in the evenings but eerie in daylight. It is possibly the bright deniers who claim that it is important to 'put by' for 'old age'. Take the lyrics of the song:

> Men grow cold
> As girls grow old
> And we all lose our charms in the end
> But square-cut or pear-shape
> These rocks don't lose their shape…

It is a great help to have a cheerful disposition, and practically proven that an ageing brain shrinks if the owner of it is unhappy. It can become one fifth smaller than a happy old brain. Mercifully this situation can be reversed with the agitation of new interests. James Spooner, one of my contributors would, however, disapprove of this theory.

My elderly uncle was feeling a little down-in-the-mouth until he bought a computer and surfed the Internet. He was in need of adventure. After a certain amount of surfing, he found romance in Thailand and spent a euphoric Christmas on a golf condominium near Bangkok. All these observations and many more have provided inspiration for the compiling of this anthology.

Recently I read somewhere or other that ageing isn't always easy – even for a cockroach. In their twilight years, apparently, they become decidedly doddery. Their joints seize up, causing them to slow down, and they have trouble walking up hills. When researchers put them on a treadmill, the adults that had reached the ripe old age of sixty weeks took around half as many steps as cockroaches in their prime. They also developed a stumbling gait, as their front foot got caught on their second leg. Curiously, however, after being decapitated the old timers developed a new lease of life – albeit brief – and were able to outrun the youngsters. In the following pages I have been offered many tips on the ageing process – although nobody has suggested decapitation.

It has been a gripping book to compile. One of the aspects of getting it together that I have enjoyed in a self-centred way is that this collection is, by necessity, somewhat personal to me. There could never be a comprehensive or complete collection of dynamic humans of over fifty years of age from around the world. That would have been no easier to assemble than a complete collection of pebbles, strands of hair, worms, trees or whatever. There are, quite simply, billions of us. The contributors to *Late Youth* are friends or relations of mine or friends or relations of friends. My brother, John Chancellor, submitted two pieces and urged me to choose between them. I couldn't – so have included them both. The same applies to my great friends Arabella Boxer, David Plante and Nigel Ryan. No point in agonizing over a decision in any of these cases.

I reached the age of sixty-nine the other day. My children and grandchildren reminded me by sending flowers, cards and marshmallows (favourites of mine). It was a mild shock to find myself entering my seventieth year, not that it made any difference to my daily life – it just sounded grisly.

It did, however, make me think a bit. I cannot be expected to compete with Kitty Carlisle Hart, aged ninety-three and the widow of the successful Broadway producer, Moss Hart. She stands on her head every day to refresh her brain and dines out every night. But here are some less strenuous Top Tips for anyone in the same boat as myself:

Be in denial. Forget your birthday. Never celebrate. I had a great friend (John Fleming, the art historian) who always treated his birthday as any other day and, by the end of his long and fruitful life, had quite forgotten when it was.

Eat and drink as little as it takes to keep body and soul together. Overdo it after the age of, say, sixty-five, and you'll wake up aching all over. That often happens to me. Abstain, and you're a chick.

Peer as seldom as possible into the looking glass.

Jilly Cooper wrote, on one of her milestone birthdays, that 'the menopause is nothing more than a pause between men' and that she intended to grow old disgracefully.

My nephew suggested that 'part of the answer is not having a pension or any other means of support. This forces one to live by one's wits whereas most pensioners become like old Labradors.'

Some are born appreciative of their entire lives from start to finish. Some have appreciation thrust upon them. I do not suggest that it is desirable to encounter crisis in middle age but, if it happens, the effect can be astonishing. At the age of sixty-one I nearly expired in a car smash. The damage to my body was dreadful, but the effect on my outlook was miraculous. Having lost half my right hand, including two fingers, while the remaining digits were crushed, I also endured a punctured lung, broken ribs, head and face cuts, pain, operations and continual giddiness, which might have constituted a setback. Oddly, as I lay in the sweltering heat in an emergency ward between plastic surgery operations, came the thrill of a narrow escape. My nine-year-old grandson wrote proudly: 'PS, I know a lady with THREE fingers missing'.

At that time it seemed to me that I might not have many months left. Quite probably, though, a good number of days. It was my duty and my need to enjoy, at least in part, each one of them. Many enjoy their later lives automatically but, with my idle nature, the urgent penny that was telling me to 'go for it' might not have dropped without a rip-roaring fright.

When my mother, a life-lover, reached the age of seventy-five, she began to fear that she was running out of time. Her solution was to rise at four a.m., read, write, garden by torchlight, play the piano, study the works of Erasmus, feed her pet sheep and still have a full day ahead of her. It didn't actually work. By lunchtime she was tired and had to spend the rest of the day in bed.

Human bodies tell the time more ruthlessly than any clock; they know best about puberty, adolescence, wrinkles, deafness, blindness and the loss and greying of hair. Since there are so many millions of these timepieces, some do – as clocks can – go wrong from time to time. When they do, they bring about premature senility and untimely crumbling of bones. The better functioning ones, however, deal solely with the passing of time. Emotions, on the other hand, they cannot control. 'The weariness, the fever and the fret', hope, fear, pain, pleasure, highs, lows, ecstasy, euphoria, despair... The clock, while dictating that the time has come for reading glasses and hearing aids, does not get them fitted, does nothing to help.

I remember a certain time of life: that moment when the euphoria of youth had passed before the acceptance of old age arrived. Panic set in. A flutter felt like the manifestation of a heart attack.

Upright in the night.

'If I'm ever going to lose weight, I'd better do it now – before it's too late.' The same applied to smoking, drinking, the improvement of behaviour. Deep down, after the age of, say, fifty, the brain is thinking to old age. Most people can be fairly sure of having passed the halfway mark. The clock, along with the wrinkles, is saying so. This should not be a problem. The world is still open. For women whose children have left home, there are many chances.

But where does the will to take these chances come from when the previous structure of life has been removed? For men in retirement, for women with no further need to 'provide'?

I have been thinking back to what could have been a golden era when I was round the fifty-mark.

The youngest of my four daughters, the last to live at home, left for an A-level boarding college. Gone were her crowds of friends; over was the constant ferrying. Gone, for the most part, was the daily pleasure of her company, involvement in homework, her tuneful singing about the house. The older girls appeared with hosts of friends at weekends. It was often hard work, and life was not empty, but times had changed.

When my songbird left home I bought a budgerigar and hung it in a glittering cage in the pantry. It didn't do much to fill the gap, and later my daughter told me that she'd been insulted to hear that she might have been replaced by a budgerigar. Strangely, though, it was the bird that committed suicide. Not me. I found it dead – upturned in its tiny drinking trough. My husband worked hard, but I was out of a job. Coming as I do from a generation of women reared in wartime, I had never trained for employment. I was fidgety, not exactly bored, but restless. There were books to read, ageing parents to visit, a garden to weed, friends to telephone. All these things I did, but there was a sense that something was past and that the next thing had not begun. Lunches and dinners are fun, but when they're over, they're over. You're back to your own devices.

The busy, busy years had passed.

I struggled along without much sense of purpose. Now, naturally, I wish I'd been warned and done better.

There were weddings, funerals and thrills. Sliding into a new era without much framework. I hand you these comments as a tip on how not to make the transition.

As we get older, the clock ticking, we can in many ways control a little more of what we are about.

A clever doctor friend of mine, now in his eighties, suggests that: 'as you get older the past gets larger and larger. The future smaller. A way to deal with this is to plan and plan ahead. Thus, the future can become almost as large as the past. Loss of memory comes simply from the kindness of nature – reducing the number of years that stretch behind in the mind.'

When I look back on my (thankfully) few years of comparative depression, I recognize with some shock that I'd been spoiled rotten.

I used to be a little shocked when I heard the maxim: 'thrifty 'til fifty then spend to the end.' I couldn't think why old people ever needed to spend a farthing. But *so* spoiled am I that there are still many things that I have failed to crack. I wish I could agree wholeheartedly that 'the best things in life are free', but as I sit on a comfortable sofa before a well-banked fire; listening to Englebert Humperdink sing 'Please Release Me' at full throttle, I know that I am happier than I would be, say, in a muddy field on this cold November day.

I am not, apparently, alone in my sybarism. Being an Oxford or a Cambridge don, I'm told, can add four years to your life. Oxford and Cambridge Universities epitomize a life of privilege; their Fellows dine off silver, live amid world-class architecture, enjoy fine wines from the college cellar and teach some of the nation's best students.

These days I'm radiant with my laptop and my many grandchildren. Nor further identity crisis. I am an ancestor. The prospect of death has ceased to be creepy. I used to quake when I saw a hearse. Now I think the coffin, lying stately within it, looks comfortable and infinitely peaceful.

I do, however, still have to confess to a certain reluctance to accept that advice to oldsters is meant for me. Today, on the wireless, I heard a soothing voice urging the elderly to wrap up warm. An icy wind was predicted from the Cairngorms. For a second I held in my mind's eye a compassionate image of tiny shrivelled figures wrapped in blankets before popping on my thermal underwear.

I read a wonderful novel by Muriel Spark some years ago. I think it was called *A Far Cry from Kensington*, and in it she included advice on how to lose weight. She said that she threw this counsel in 'for the price of the book'. With my anthology I do the same. I give you details, including the telephone number, of Glin Castle: surely the most comfortable, exotic, historic and heavenly hotel in the world. I also give you details of Jonathan Guinness's yoga classes. He looks terrifically fit. I urge you to visit Sudely Castle; David Tang's glamorous shops and clubs; buy your antiquarian books from John Chancellor or David Batterham; get your library catalogued by Vanessa Williams Ellis, your garden designed by Roddy Llewellyn or Tim Leese; read the latest books by the thrilling authors who have contributed here, and so on throughout these enlightening pages.

One further thing about the book. There may seem to be an odd discrepancy between the many 'potted biographies'. I have an explanation for this. Some contributors have sent succinct descriptions of themselves that they are happy to see in print. Others have been more bashful, and I have had to use my imagination and powers of description when concocting them. I would like to thank every old codger represented here for sharing their secrets, and I also thank Ellen Ann Hopkins for starting me off on the venture – for having had the original idea and for introducing me to Gary Pulsifer.

Finally, if I die and have not got around to mentioning this in my will, I would like a good organist to play 'Wish Me Luck As You Wave Me Goodbye' at my funeral and for my four daughters and nine grandchildren (or more if they come along) to sing it very, very loudly. I would like it even better if my husband Nicholas and I were to die simultaneously and that they sing 'Wish *us* luck...' instead of just 'me'.

THE FASCINATING MYSTERY OF EXISTENCE

FOR me the most testing thing about growing older is the effort of keeping the body and wits in good working order. Yoga (for the over-fifties), sessions with the osteopath and costly expeditions between the nutritionist and my local organic emporium, stocking up on vitamins, supplements and gorgeous-looking (and tasting) vegetables take up a great part of my weekly visits to London. Otherwise, I am for the time being in harness at Sudeley, despite rumours of a takeover by my grown-up children, Henry and Mollie and their families.

Sudeley has fascinated, challenged, maddened and at times almost finished me off ever since I was first introduced to the family property some forty years ago by my then future husband Mark Brocklehurst. The castle and estate had been purchased in the early nineteenth century as a romantic and ghostly ruin by his enthusiastic forebears, the Dent brothers: wealthy glove-makers from Worcester who, having commenced an ambitious restoration effort, died. It has thereafter mystified and tested the stamina of the next four generations of owners as to how to cope with it. An impractical building to live in and aggravated by neglect during two world wars, resulting in the selling-off of most of its supporting land, it came to me on the sad and untimely death of Mark in 1972. In a sorry state of repair and producing little income, being made open to the public seemed the likely route to recovery. This was certainly helped by the castle's special charm and the illustrious roll call of former residents and celebrity owners – such as Richard III, Henry VIII, Katherine Parr and others – to entice and entertain our visitors. Sudeley is a place where fantasies can come to life. Immersing myself in its intriguing thousand-year history and producing an ever-changing tableau of amusements to satisfy the annual 'what's new this season?' requirements of the coach operators is a demanding but perpetually interesting task. Reclaiming and restoring the once regal gardens has been a dream project, particularly – not having the gift myself – working with some of the most talented and renowned garden gurus. One can't complain about living and working in such magical surroundings with wonderful treasures. However, I've done my fair share of whingeing over it. Try as we may, I am stymied by the ever-demanding needs of the old place. Successful as the tourist trade would seem, it is fickle and creates new economic problems of wear and tear, bureaucratic interference and unsettling protests from the locals.

A few years ago I was diagnosed with chronic fatigue: a perplexing condition for many doctors who can't see the point of it as it doesn't respond to conventional drugs treatment. I subsequently headed down the alternative path, a long, winding road but nevertheless a major eye-opener and an introduction agency to new – or should I say rediscovered? – ideas of healing, living and seeing things in a different way. I discovered an eclectic world of good people, cranks and inspired, learned voices of wisdom and sanity. Now virtually recovered and happily redirected, I would love to have more time to support the work and visions of the leading thinkers in these fields of research and teaching. Unfortunately, Sudeley doesn't allow much time for other causes, but we could always encourage the mountain to come to Muhammad. We have already gone organic in the garden and kitchen and have plans to convert more of the estate. If alternative methods could rejuvenate me, why couldn't they do the same for crumbling stones? An injection of new and radical ideas is needed to help Sudeley adapt to a new age. Curiously, the castle has suffered the ravages of war and disgrace under its male proprietors and seemingly comes to life and grows peaceful when under the care of women. Perhaps the next generation will have the answer, as it will belong equally to Henry and Mollie. Or will it be time for the old Dents' heirs to fold their tent and for new blood to take over? Sudeley has never been the exclusive seat of one noble family whose continuing support it could rely on. It has had to adapt in order to survive, and the ebb and flow of its fortunes have, to a large extent, mirrored those of the country at large. Whatever fate decrees, Sudeley will survive; and I will continue to support holistic health and the spiritual and ecological philosophies through which all is linked. The best part of getting older is that I enjoy the given things most: the beauty of nature, old friends and new friends, family and particularly the adorable grandchildren. For what it's worth, my useful tips to those with age concerns are: eat health-giving and organic food, take long, lung-expanding walks, preferably with a dog, enjoy your nearest and dearest to the full and make space from the exhausting and questionable values of our materialistic culture to explore the fascinating mystery of existence.

JACK BAER
GROWING PAINS

I AM eighty. I keep working and go to my office five days a week from ten to five-thirty. I believe activity keeps me young and useful and stops me thinking that I am grown up. To be grown up must be boring: you have nothing to aim for. To my question, 'Do you feel grown up?' which I put to my dear friend Denis Mahon after his ninety-fourth birthday, his immediate reply was: 'Of course not, I still feel about eighteen.'

My short-term memory cannot be replied upon, and so I have a pocket full of lists, which I try to remember to look at every half hour or so. On the other hand, my long-term memory is quite good, and some of the incidents highlighting age are very clear indeed, and, as time passes, they come to mind more and more often.

On my first day at pre-preparatory school a larger, stronger and rather intimidating boy gripped my arms and stood on my shoes into which my feet had been shoehorned – most carefully – by my governess only an hour before my apprehensive arrival at the school gate.

'My name is Phillip. Are your shoes new?' he asked.

'Yes,' I replied apologetically and added, to show I was capable of uttering more than one word under interrogation, 'Yes, very.' The next question came fast:

'How old are you?'

'Six,' I said.

'I am seven,' he said with a broad grin to which I bravely announced:

'But I'll catch you up.'

Ten years later in 1940, when my older brother and I were ready to leave home and go to see the Crazy Gang at the Victoria Palace, we stood at the foot of our mother's bed, where she lay ill with 'flu, to say goodnight. Both of us were over six foot tall and my brother in the uniform of a lieutenant in the Royal Artillery and about to be sent to join the Eighth Army in North Africa.

'Do be careful crossing Victoria Street in the blackout,' she said most seriously.

'Of course we will,' my brother said with great kindness, as his hand patted the holster of his service revolver while we hid our smiles.

The third incident, which frequently comes to mind, took place at the start of the D-Day landings on the Normandy beaches where, while in the RAF, I was serving in a Combined Operations Unit. Early that morning, before any of the landing craft started the assault, I stood on deck during a few moments off-duty with a small group of older, more experienced men and watched the awesome bombardment. While I saw it as a child might view a splendid firework display, those near me were grey-faced, seeing something totally different: danger, mutilation and death, all of which they had already witnessed earlier at Anzio or Salerno. I was still a boy believing that nothing could happen to me, while they were fully aware that this moment might well be our last.

After Normandy and then a year in the Pacific, I returned to London, was demobilized and went home. I made enquiries about old friends including the seven-year-old who had stood on my shoes.

'How's Phillip?' I asked those of my pre-prep school days. They told me that as a pilot in the RAF he had been shot down and killed just before the end of the war.

Oh, God! So I *had* caught him up. Soon, many of my juniors will catch me up and overtake me but, like Phillip, I will never know.

CHRISTOPHER BALFOUR
SIXTY-THREE AND STILL TRUCKING

I SPENT years on being congratulated on 'still looking thirty' and loving it. I could drink the young under the table and dance till dawn and still be the life and soul of the lunch party the following day. Alas, the party was over towards my late fifties: energy levels down, a new feeling called 'exhaustion', and – horror of horrors – I had to admit that I could not drink as much as I used to.

The negatives are, of course, ghastly: my ever-increasing deafness, stiffness and, worst of all, lack of any reliable memory bank. The only thing to do is to think positive. I now refuse to worry about any of the following:

Being late

Being caught in traffic jams

Missing meetings

Missing flights or trains (there is always the next one)

Unpaid bills

Ever since I was at Oxford, I knew that my favourite pastime was 'wasting' time and drinking and laughing with my closest friends. There have been moments in my life when I cut down on this delightful pastime, and it is a joy now to do little else. They too have reached old age, and therefore we can all forgive each other for repeating ourselves, spilling red wine regularly over each other's tablecloths and clothes, forgetting overcoats, umbrellas and spectacles in each other's houses and needing constant reminders of luncheon dates and forgiving each other when yet again one of us has made a cock-up. It doesn't matter because when it comes off it's more fun than ever.

Not hearing is a nuisance, and one's back preventing one from carrying one's own luggage is a bore, but there are compensations for the white-haired, stooped figure one has become – it is extraordinary how often people help you. My greatest coup was in Malaga airport, where the walk from the aeroplane to the exit is even longer than at Gatwick; a charming man with a buggy stopped to pick up me and the friend I was with. At first I was indignant, and when I explained that no, we did not order a buggy he replied that he knew that but we looked as if we needed help. What an enjoyable luxury it was! Another time, a nice attendant from the airport shop chased me thirty yards to give me back my passport and boarding card (what would I have done when I reached the gate without them?) and people are very kind about reading things to one when one cannot find one's spectacles.

I refused to take the advice of those who love me ('you must look after yourself', 'you must take things easier', 'you must try to slow down') on the basis of 'bop until you drop'. I intend to continue with the daily Martini and claret with lunch and dinner and to go to any party I might still be asked to. But one great confession: this life cannot be led without an essential ingredient: the two-hour siesta some time between three and six p.m. Miss it at my peril – I shall be cantankerous, overdo the drink and have a row in the evening; but after a siesta I can still pretend I'm in my twenties until dawn.

This Stretch Of Life

I ALWAYS thought 'second childhood' meant the mewling and puking stage, but I was wrong. It must surely mean the bit when you enjoy excessively and ridiculously recreating your first childhood with your grandchildren. I mean you actually get chickens for the first time in your life aged – in my case, sixty-six – in order to see the children enjoying collecting the eggs for the first time and watching the chicks hatch out. Then you find that you're enjoying it far more than they are, as they're worrying whether Angelina Ballerina has got muddy or something. The same goes for flying a kite or sloshing paint around or damming the stream. Definitely more fun now. It's we too who are constantly amazed at the intoxicating beauty of nature, even though we've experienced the changing seasons for many years, while the first-timers hardly notice it.

The lack of deference towards the old – although very unfair because it is, after all, our turn – makes life with the first-timers much funnier. Frank (aged five) marching into my bathroom the other day: 'Oh hello, Gran, are you doing a poo or a pee?' 'Luckily for you, Frank, a pee.' 'Oh, d'you know, Gran, girls do a pee out of their bottoms but boys do it from their willies?' (Demonstrating) 'Did you know that, Gran?' 'No, Frank, really?'

It's very cruel that human beings have evolved, unlike any of the other animals, to the point where they are conscious of their own mortality but powerless to avoid it. What a recipe for a life of terror! When I recently thought I might be going to die very soon, I realized for the first time something perfectly obvious. Death is terribly sad, but if it's you who has died or stopped living, you won't be the one who has to go through the awful misery of grieving that comes afterwards.

I love this stretch of life. Just enough grist to the mill in the way of work, and then more times when you have the new luxury of being able to go on doing the thing you want to do for as long as you want without having to stop and do something you have to do. I wish it wouldn't go past quite so quickly. It feels like it's the last bit of the bathwater suddenly speeding up and gurgling down the plughole just when it seemed one was beginning to get the hang of things.

DAVID BATTERHAM

CRUMPLED GABARDINE MAC

WHEN I stayed with my grandmother in 1943, my brother and I made friends with an old lady who lived in an almshouse nearby. She looked like a witch, as she had only one huge tooth. But we were not frightened of her because Grandpa also only had one tooth. We gazed at her in awe, as she was said to be ninety-six.

Later, I wished I had been more curious about her. She could have given us her views on Disraeli, recalled the Relief of Mafeking bonfires or the coronation of Edward VII, shared her thoughts on Mrs Pankhurst.

But even if I had been precocious and cheeky enough aged ten to have asked her about these things, it would have been no use. She was already gaga.

Now I find that I shall soon be ninety-six myself. *Very* soon, if time speeds up over the next twenty-five years at the same accelerating rate it has done for the twenty-five just gone.

I never got to grips with Einstein's theory – time being bent and the future having already happened and so on – perhaps the phenomenon of time changing speed as one gets older was part of it. It may explain why we gradually forget how old we have become.

When my mother was eighty-nine, for example, she said to me: 'I've worked hard all my life, and I don't want the taxman to have any of my money.' I thought at the time that this was strange because, although she had left school and started work when she was fifteen, she had married my father when she was twenty-five and never had another job. Now I can see how those sixty-four years flashed by and had little temporal validity compared to the ten long years in her job.

I have not so far been tempted (or needed?) to wear make-up or a corset to improve my posture (like the elderly CO of my regiment, I remember).

Some old men do seem to worry a lot about their hair. I do remember when most wigs were a metallic ginger colour – perhaps they were free NHS wigs. They had a one-size-fits-all look, standing out an inch all round from very bare necks. One of my sharpest memories of visiting America is of a bar in San Antonio where I fell in with a completely bald and very gloomy man. He told me that his mother was always on at him to get a wig. Her latest plea was to get him to wear one at least on Sundays, for her sake, to church.

Not long ago, staying with friends near Bath, I tried an experiment. After shaving and cleaning my teeth, I looked at myself in the bathroom mirror and took my hairbrush and dipped it in the basin and tried to brush my hair forward over my bald head in a sort of Roman emperor look. I arrived at the breakfast table expecting a screech of laughter. Nothing! Presumably they bit their lips and thought: 'Poor old David'.

So you see I am not sure about the advantages and disadvantages, the pleasures and drawbacks of old age.

I still have a number of my faculties, though my memory is now unreliable. I can still just see that. I do sometimes worry that if ever I decide to take the big jar of pills I will have forgotten where I have hidden it.

The other day I caught sight of a tall, balding, grey-haired man in a crumpled gabardine mac and muffler reflected in a shop window in Westbourne Grove, and for a moment I wondered how my father could have reappeared. He died the other day – in January 1980.

ANTHONY BLOND

THIS IS FOR MEN

THIS is for men over seventy, irritable, no longer able to carry their own luggage, people like me – since a bypass; prone to tears, the result, according to Anne Chisholm, of the heart having been knifed – though others not in this category may look in on it, as it were. Your second wife should be quite a bit younger than you, with enough of her own money to buy her own clothes and something over for joint treats. You will grow to like some of her friends, which will keep you in companionship as yours die off. Old and new friendships should be lubricated with postcards and telephone calls, now so cheap that it doesn't matter where you live. (Calls to Australia are down to two pence for a minute, and there is a new communications company that charges nothing at all, their profits coming from a modest one-off registration fee.)

You can only live in England if you are rich enough to buy space to keep the rest of the population at a distance, which is why I live in France in a seventeenth-century house with twenty-three rooms that costs the same as a one-bedroom studio off the Fulham Road. The meals in country restaurants can be excellent and cheap, the roads are empty and the hospital service *sans pareil.*

Your second home should be in the Third World. I recommend Sri Lanka, where Laura – second wife – bought a house twenty-five years ago. We have a cook, her athletic son who massages me and acts as houseboy, a gardener, a night watchman (obligatory), a man who comes every morning to check the pool and a lady who tends the spice garden, *ci devant* tennis court which I can no longer use as such. Totted up, they all cost as much as a London char. The average Sri Lankan earns in a week the same as a US worker does in an hour.

This sounds like the life of Riley (who *was* Riley?), but, in fact, my main support is from my old age pension – and my lack of affluence from having signed a joint and several guarantee, which no one should ever do. I had offended Messrs C Hoare and Co., who nearly foreclosed, by dedicating a book to them and was rescued by my brother. I know some people who spend a thousand pounds on a suit, but my best jacket, made in Poland, was lurking in a thrift shop in Minnesota and cost seven dollars; and my second best, admired by a wealthy nobleman, who was staying here the other day, Laura bought for twenty-five francs in the local charity shop. To touch on less worldly matters, I pray twice a day from my prayer book, bits of whose Hebrew I have taught myself to pronounce, and I practise mild yoga exercises, including one for the eyes.

One final tip is from Robert Kee, the most handsome eighty-five-year-old in the kingdom, who told me that if anyone our age walked from one room to the other and could remember why, there must be something wrong with him, which should comfort your contributor, the distinguished Isabel Colegate, harassed in this area by the awful Janet.

John Bowes Lyon
Not So Old

THERE are those who are born world-weary, and those whose youthful spirits always make their company a joy.

There is, of course, no secret elixir to keep us young: certainly not endless workouts in gyms, laps in horrid swimming pools nor injections of monkey glands (such as Dr Niehans gave to Somerset Maugham and others). Who wants to have a baby face at the age of ninety or a chin joined to the knee?

When I was young, today's 'miracle medicines' were yet to be invented, and what is now considered a young age was then thought of as the finishing straight of life.

Now that longevity has been prolonged by science, old age does not seem to be quite as overwhelming a prospect as once it was. There are endless varieties of entertainment on television, and communication is far easier and more affordable than it was in the past. This helps to keep the spirits up and reduce the fear of loneliness.

I believe in the old-fashioned recipe of a cocktail of good company and plenty of laughter as the most effective way of staying young, which is not to say that a genuine cocktail goes amiss from time to time.

A sense of humour counts for almost everything. The English are good at jokes, whether they be Brighton Pier, lavatorial or from the stable. 'I don't like 'is 'ock or 'is ass or anything that is 'is' still sends me into fits.

Lord David Cecil maintained that: 'Happiness must come unsought in this hard world; pursued, it eludes us.' Too true.

Although the young cheer us all with promise of the future, it is often the senior citizens of this world whose cheerfulness and spirit keep our lives going merrily along.

> Life is mostly froth and bubble
> Two things stand like stone
> Kindness in another's trouble
> Courage in your own.
> – A. L. Gordon

ARABELLA BOXER
LATE YOUTH

GROWING older, for me, has inevitably become linked with a solitary life. When I began to live alone for the first time, approaching fifty, I was quite looking forward to it. But as so often happens, everything turned out differently from what I had expected. The leisure to read and reread books, listen to music and to enjoy my sunny flat almost immediately became a bore. The amusing hours I had expected to spend reliving old memories were merely tedious, often even painful. I soon discovered that leisure, as an end in itself, is not worth much; it is only in relation to work that it can be enjoyed. Slowly I learned to re-evaluate my life, to learn what made me happy and to stop feeling restless.

About ten years after starting to live alone I gave up working, and the same pattern repeated itself. For a few days I enjoyed waking up each morning without a deadline hanging over my head. It was fun cooking whatever I wanted, without having to take notes and invent recipes. But again the positive benefits quickly wore off, and I was left with an aimless feeling that I had accomplished nothing at the end of each week.

The answer, for me, seems to be constant activity, so long as it does not involve stress in any form. In the intervening years, I have kept tropical fish, cultivated Japanese bonsai, done courses in such things as Modern Greek, Japanese and American History, let rooms to visiting doctors, learned to use a computer and digital camera and made annual visits to New York.

All worked for a time; only two have lasted. I never grow tired of fooling around on my computer, while the visits to New York are a constant delight. My American mother died eight years ago, and after her death I began to spend time visiting my American cousins, looking up the houses in the city where the family used to live and researching their forebears in the New York libraries.

I went to New York for the first time after the war, when I was twelve, and the sheer hedonistic pleasure of it after life in the north of Scotland and blitzed London was unbelievable. I had no memory of pre-war life in Britain, and the fun and gaiety of New York – the food, the shops, the clothes – were astounding. There must be something therapeutic about revisiting places where one has been happy as a child, for a little of this happiness returns each time I go back.

Although I have lived in London for almost sixty years, the city has no family connections for me. My father was the first in his family to buy a London house, which he only did to please my mother and rarely visited himself. In New York, on the other hand, where my mother's family have lived for over two hundred years, both the Washington Square area and the Upper East Side are filled with echoes of their past history. My grandparents moved uptown in 1902, the year before my mother was born, and built the house in East 66th Street where Andy Warhol later lived until he died. After she married, they moved further uptown, to an apartment overlooking the Reservoir in Central Park, while my great aunt Olivia lived on the corner of Madison Avenue and 72nd Street, which is now Polo Ralph Lauren. All these things remind me of my American heritage, which I find curiously reassuring, and of the fun I used to have in New York when I was young. Then the sunny mood returns.

ONE DECISION I NEVER REGRETTED

ONE of the disadvantages of making something you love into your life's work is that it soon ceases to be enjoyable. This must be true of food writing as it is of many other things, for the fun of doing something purely for pleasure is lost. Trying to invent recipes without plagiarizing other people's, testing and retesting dishes, weighing and reweighing all the ingredients, keeping notes and having to eat dishes when one has no appetite for them: all these things can become trying. I was once asked to do a whole book – a short one, but still – for Sainsburys on pâtés. Now pâtés are something I don't much like at the best of times, and the thought of having to make – and eat – some sixty different pâtés appalled me. Although initially anxious not to offend them by refusing, in case I was never asked again (I wasn't), that was one decision I never regretted. Having to produce fourteen recipes for chocolate dishes for *Vogue* was enough for my liver to rebel and put me off chocolate for life.

I stopped writing for *Vogue* in 1991. When my last book was published, seven years later, I was sixty-five. My mother died the following year, and I inherited a small amount of money, enough to bring in just about what I had been earning. So I was free to stop work and do what I liked.

The end result was less enjoyable than I'd expected. Work had become my raison d'être, and without it I felt lost. Although it was wonderful to be free of deadlines and all the related anxiety, I missed the sense of achievement that was the end result. I became bored and depressed by doing nothing. In the end I realized that constant activity was the only hope if I was to stay happy, so long as its form did not involve stress of any kind. After a while I rediscovered cooking and, as in the case of Maeterlink's bluebird, I found the answer close to home.

Cookery proved to be one of the very best and most rewarding of accomplishments. Whereas before, cooking had almost always been associated with some form of duty, either feeding the family or writing for books and for the media, now I am free to do it for my own pleasure. No longer do I have to have dinner parties. My table only holds five or six at the most, but two or three is my preferred number. Nothing is much trouble on such a small scale, be it cleaning mussels, shelling peas, peeling Jerusalem artichokes or making spring rolls.

Also quite enjoyable, although I am often too lazy to do it, is cooking for oneself. Here I tend to do very simple, quick dishes, rather like those of my childhood: grilled lamb cutlets with carrots and leeks; boiled Patna rice with sprouting broccoli and grilled tomatoes; a small sirloin steak, grilled, with a baked potato and a green salad. One of the simplest and best dishes, for when I am alone and cold, tired or ill, is one I found in a book of Claudia Roden's some years ago. I adapted it, inevitably, and have now come to think of it as my own, the original having been lost without trace.

Rice with Egg Yolk

90g/3oz Patna rice
1 egg yolk
7g/1/4oz butter, cut in small bits
Sea salt and black pepper

Boil the rice as usual, then drain well and tip into a small bowl. While it is still very hot, stir in the egg yolk and beat with a fork. Then stir in the bits of butter, adding plenty of coarse sea salt and freshly ground black pepper. Eat immediately, with a spoon.

Melvyn Bragg
Ageing Is So Odd

AGEING is so odd. Suddenly I'm sixty-five and yet yesterday I was fourteen, two weeks ago I was twenty-seven and only a month ago I turned forty. The clichés rain down. Where did it all go? Why does Christmas come around once a week? The man in the street was right all the time with his implacable placard: THE END IS NIGH.

But how very strange and surely not for me, we all think, armoured as we are in anti-death confidence that defies the only certainty in life. How odd to hear a creak as you go up the stairs and to realize it is the knees and not the stairs. Even at beach cricket the younger lot long ago were making allowances. We slow down everywhere but inside, surely the sap will rise as before... Won't it?

And are the gilded promises of age turning out to be false? Am I – are you – wiser? No. All passion spent? No. Serene, secure, above the struggle? Not really. The usual jumble goes on. Intensified, I suspect in the case of my generation since we are the first to be (mostly) fit enough to govern ourselves for longer than ever but generally considered unfit to govern anybody or anything else.

But the oddness is the most striking feature. Who is this ageing person walking wearily and eyeing up the steep stairs with anxiety? It isn't, is it? Surely not... It can't be...

HARRIET BRIDGEMAN
WHAT KEEPS ONE YOUNG?

WHAT keeps one young? I suspect that it is partly never having time to think about getting old – and what is old apart from creaking bones and lethargy spawned by lack of interest in life?

If one is fortunate, as I am, to have lived life at a gallop, there seems no reason to change step – providing, of course, that one's energy and good health remain constant.

I started the Bridgeman Art Gallery over thirty years ago and had no thought of it growing at the pace it has. During these years I have travelled the world, searching through pictures and collections. The adventure is still on, and long may it continue – keeping me young and most certainly happy.

Museum conferences in Melbourne, New Orleans and St Louis, driving into the outback to meet aboriginal artists, dancing on paddle steamers, marching in Mardi Gras parades: all of these experiences have provided the unexpected bonus of working with museum collections. The variety, the new interests and adventures are supremely life enhancing and guard one against old age with far greater success than a daily dose of pills.

Last year I travelled to see fourteen museums in Brazil in eleven days with a delightful young man from our New York office. When not acting as my interpreter, my colleague was investigating the respective merits of junior curators. His enthusiasm was abated when he was told that cosmetic surgery in Brazil had become such a fine art that seventy-year-old women were now parading as thirty-year-olds. It is comforting to know that if the desire to remain young and the budget is there, the clock can be put back.

The fact that my husband – now in his seventies and busier than ever – supports the theory that seventy is the new sixty.

As we get older, people tend to ask the same question: 'When do you plan to retire?' My answer is that, if you are doing something that you enjoy, what is the incentive to stop? I firmly believe that the busier you are the younger you remain.

Lucy Bridgewater

Always The Wrong Age

My MOTHER, Mary Malcolm, was one of the first 'Forces Sweethearts' and was more than aware that her grandmother, Lily Langtry, the Jersey Lily, was the forever-famous beauty. To some extent Mary, self-centred and extremely pretty, traded on this: certainly did not allow it to be a hindrance to her career. She was an early television announcer and, when I was small, used to introduce me to her colleagues, saying: 'This is Lucy. She's seven.' But I wasn't. I was only six at the time.

I was always the wrong age. When I was fourteen I became hooked on staying with a family in France. Thérèse was one of the many *au pair* girls my mother enrolled to dish out the spaghetti. She was sixteen when I was fourteen. She came from a large family who lived in a small town near Lille, and I thought she was perfect. I used to go with her and her family for holidays near Le Touquet where I met a boy who always wanted to dance with me at the sailing club. He was nineteen and asked me how old I was. I refused to tell him right up to the time when, eventually, our dancing days came to an end. Since then I always longed to be older than I was, but now I wish I'd grown more gently into the right age. Now that the truth is out.

Although it came as a surprise, I love collecting my pension. At first it was a shock. I went to a ladies lunch party – all shoulder pads and lipstick. I'm told that I arrived with a face of thunder, for nobody had questioned my bus pass or suggested that I'd stolen it. It's marvellous being a pensioner: like being tipped. I had only ever before been tipped when I worked as a waitress, perhaps when I was fourteen pretending to be sixteen.

When I became eligible for my pension there were problems because my mother had never kept any record of my birth. I searched through all her files and made inquiries at Somerset House. Nobody had any idea who I was. After complicated inquiries I got my pension book and a huge backlog of cash. With it I bought a rotovator for my kitchen garden. This coincided with my being unable to dig it by myself.

My identity, as well as my age, has always been open to debate. I have in recent years had many brushes with death: an eight-hour brain operation as well as two goes of cancer and two courses of chemotherapy. I went totally bald and was constantly mistaken for Judi Dench who has a chubby face and very short hair. I didn't mind this as I admire her greatly. To begin with I wore a bandana attached to a silk scarf and a false fringe from a shop in Kensington High Street. It was hot and itchy and foul and one day, at Pisa airport, I ripped it off at customs and arrived at the house of friends who were in the middle of giving a lunch party, with not a hair on my head. A tiny woman came up and said: 'Congratulations on your performance as Iris.'

Sometimes people said: 'You're so brave. We've always wanted to try shaving our heads.' Was I to say 'I've just had fucking cancer'?

I'm not sure if I've changed much. I'm as uncharitable as ever, but I appreciate everything more. I have been incredibly well cared for by my husband. All the same, I'm rather pleased he's lost his passport. It gives me a teeny-weeny advantage. He's happy that my health is restored and tells me I've been brave, but I know that there hasn't been an alternative. It is excellent to be alive.

GEORGIA CAMPBELL
I Do Not Regret The Passing Of The Years

WHEN I was younger, I could not understand why my seniors bemoaned the fact that youth is wasted on the young. Now that I am over fifty, however, I appreciate what they meant. If one could have the skin and figure in maturity that one had in one's youth, while retaining all the wisdom and comfort in your own skin that are by-products of getting older (if you do it right and don't squander life's lessons), one would indeed have it all. However, life dictates that we can never have it all, and I for one do not regret the passing of the years. I love seeing young and pretty girls riding the crest of the wave as they head towards the feast on the beach and always remind them to enjoy it while it lasts; for catholic appeal doesn't continue forever, even if a woman who keeps her face and figure – and who, even more importantly, has a vital personality – will always have admirers, irrespective of her age. I also love the easiness with which one rides the waves of life as one ages. Having survived so much, one is invariably relaxed about the latest tsunami that threatens (but doesn't quite) take one out to sea.

The years provide riches and add a dimension not only to one's identity but also to one's relationships in a way that only time can do; and I feel lucky to be in my fifties right now, with all the advances that there are going on in the medical and health industries. To be over fifty and healthy nowadays – as I am – is to be young enough to enjoy the residue of youth but old enough to sup on the fruit of age – for the fifties are to our times what the thirties were to earlier ages, and in some ways we as a civilization have managed to extend our peak years for at least a decade as no other has done before.

On Growing Old

ONE of the poignant things about growing old is that whoever's doing it is the person least likely to recognize what's going on. He may become uneasily aware of his increasing physical frailty, he may even start to fret about the wrinkles that he sees in the mirror; but he basically doesn't feel very different from what he has ever felt.

Alas, it is unusual for a man (I am thinking only about men here) to grow calmer or wiser with age. More often, he is prey to the same anxieties and vulnerable to the same emotions that afflicted him in his youth. It is those younger than he who want him to feel old.

In my case, the first intimations of the onset of old age came in my mid-fifties (I am now sixty-five) when I returned to London after living for a time in New York. I got a job on the *Sunday Telegraph* and was horrified when one of the younger journalists addressed me as 'Sir' and held open a door to let me through.

Worse happened when I was travelling to work on the Underground in the rush hour. I was standing up, vaguely eyeing a very pretty girl sitting below me, when she abruptly rose to her feet and offered me her seat. It was very decent of her, but I was indignant. I rejected her offer tetchily.

For some years now I have been writing a weekly column for the Saturday edition of the *Guardian*. It used to have just my name at the top of it, but recently it was decided that it should be given a new title. Would I mind, I was asked politely, if it were called 'Guide to Age'? I said I didn't, but I suppose that secretly I did.

I hadn't thought that there had been anything old-sounding about my column. But maybe my employers felt that the readers of the *Guardian*'s excellent but youth-orientated *Weekend* magazine (all newspapers are obsessed with appealing to youth) needed to be given a reason for the employment of someone so old.

Francis Macdonald Cornford, an eminent classicist and philosopher, wrote early in the last century that when you approach the threshold of old age, you will hear 'the roar of a ruthless multitude of young men in a hurry. You may perhaps grow aware of what they are in a hurry to do. They are in a hurry to get you out of the way.'

That is a sad thought, but it has some truth in it. You may be doing whatever you do just as well as you ever did, and the young may even recognize this, but they are eager to get their turn to do it instead of you. It is in the interests of the young to decide that you are past it, whether that is true or not.

The best choice for the ageing is not to resist these pressures but to find an occupation – gardening, writing, property development or whatever – that does not depend for its pursuit upon the patronage of those younger than themselves.

John Chancellor
Youthful Dotage

Some people have told me that my looks belie my advanced years and that I appear to be more youthful than my father at the same age. Let us assume this to be true.

My father was of slight build and was healthy; he was never unwell, and he therefore took it particularly badly when his brain stopped functioning at a relatively early age.

I, on the other hand, am used to ill health. An enlarged prostate prevents me from emptying my bladder. The elegant wine glasses my son Eddy gave me for Christmas are being put to a use that might surprise him: that of miniature urinals. I make urgent use of them every few minutes. This does not worry me in the least: since the age of seventeen, I've had several hundred urethral operations to open up my bladder, and I'm very happy to be able to urinate at all, even with an awkward frequency.

How does all this explain my comparative 'youthfulness'? Some have spotted in me the continual existence of a certain sexual and/or emotional drive, an unawareness of age, a taste for 'slumming it'. Given my poverty, this latter predilection is fortunate. Others speak of my wish to give people 'pleasure', maybe in the theatrical sense of wanting to entertain.

I have only to look in the mirror to realize the inexorability of 'senescence': a French, but also English word, for growing old, used repeatedly by Simone de Beauvoir in *La Vieillesse*. This spectacle of senescence causes contradictory feelings within me; the sight of my next-door neighbour, only a few years older than me, '*ce petit vieillard maigre et pitoyable*', semi-demented, makes me feel youthful, debonair and organized; and I forget the 'truth' of the mirror on the wall. He is looked after by 'carers' around the clock and revels in having his bottom wiped and his face shaved.

Braveheart, (another neighbour) on the other hand, young, exuberant and lusty, is a reminder of the mirror's 'truth'. However, my great age – forty years older than he – does not worry him; and I tend, therefore, to ignore the mirror's warning. I behave as his contemporary, spending hours in pubs, generally in nearby St Neots, with him and his mates, most of them of low-grade, London overspill origin, trying to remember to lace every sentence with the expletive 'fuck'. He likes to send me off to buy sexual accessories, such as vibrating dildos and deluxe fantasy sex dolls. My latest acquisition is Sexy Sharon: 'You can have me in any way and every way. I love every act of sex that you can think of… Sharon.' Sharon is enormously tall – getting on for six foot – with orifices galore. Braveheart suspects, rightly, that I bought the cheapest version I could find, and he wants one more sophisticated, versatile and expensive. You could regard all this as an heroic effort to combat old age, or you could say it's a brutal reminder of the 'senescence' of my organs.

My Cat And My Diabetes

LIKE many a spinster and widow, I have a cat as companion in my dotage. His name is Punktli; he is white with large black markings. He was given to me by a German philosopher in Cambridge (hence his name, meaning roughly a small cat with spots, or a cat with small spots) a couple of years ago. From the word 'go' he was savage, frightened and impossible – in fact, feral or feline. He spent the first month cowering behind a bookcase, emerging briefly for meals and lashing out with his paw if I tried to stroke him.

That was two years ago. In the meantime, Punktli has acquired some of those attributes which are meant to make cats 'lovable', such as a beautiful face, dignity, character, independence and so on. I wait to hear the squeaky click of the cat-flap, the patter of little feet, the peremptory 'Meow!' demanding to be fed. None of this has yet stirred me to eulogize him in verse, *à la* T. S. Eliot or Swinburne, as in. the latter's 'To A Cat' (1895):

> Stately, kindly, lordly friend
> Condescend
> Here to sit by me...

Punktli still lashes out, drawing blood on exposed parts of my body, but his intentions are now friendly, not hostile. I mentioned this to my sister, Susanna. She has no use for cats: 'There's no point in these animals; they cannot wash up or post a letter, they just mutilate birds and cover the whole place with their hair. I defy you to put them to a practical use!'

How do I respond to this challenge? I think I've found a way!

Last year in the Cromwell Hospital, while lying exhausted after an Oesophageal Dilatation, or maybe it was a Flexible Sigmoidoscopy – I forget, I've had so many of these fucking things (I'm told the word 'fuck' is now *de rigeur* if a writer wants to be 'with it') – a Jewish endocrinologist crept slyly into my room, pricked my limp hand and disappeared. Next day I was informed that I was officially diabetic; they gave me a diabetic kit, complete with lancet, blood glucometer and 'Home Monitoring Diary', with orders to record my blood glucose level at the same time every day, or else! Since then I have tried over and over again to get drops of blood out of my fingers from the bottom up. I left my hands in near boiling water then pricked with the lancet, but no bloody blood came out. I was at my wits' end. Then I remembered my sister's challenge about making practical use of Punktli. This led me to the blood that flows from his gashes. You can guess the rest; I've had no further problem in getting blood out of my hands, arms or whatever part of my body he chooses to lacerate. I keep my monitoring diary up-to-date, although Punktli cannot do much about the frighteningly high glucose levels.

Punktli still often refuses to recognize me by day but, in the stillness of the night, he leaps onto my bed and energetically kneads my groin with his paws. They tell me that kittens do this to their mothers to make the milk flow. Perhaps I should get rid of Punktli; cats are, after all, companions of old age, which I'm supposed to be combating.

ROBIN CHANCELLOR
ON GROWING OLD

GROWING old, like life itself, is a mixed blessing, depending largely on one's circumstances. I once met an elderly American lady whose visiting card had printed on the back: 'Do not resent growing old. It is a privilege denied to many.' But she was still hale and hearty; I wondered how she would feel if she was bedridden or severely disabled. I have so far kept hale myself (I am not the hearty type) so don't have much to complain of, not even about my circumstances, which are comfortable. Indeed, environmentally perfect. Forty-five years ago in a derelict state I bought and converted a Palladian chapel dated 1630 with fine views and many peacocks. I still live in it and could hardly wish for more.

I never really gave much thought to the ageing process until I hit eighty and suddenly realized that I was way down the far side of the hill. Up to then if, as happened rarely, somebody offered me their seat on the Underground, I was as likely to feel insulted (do I look so very decrepit?) as grateful. I still have all my hair and walk reasonably tall, so...

There are, of course, many drawbacks, but none worthy of resentment. Time seems to accelerate in proportion to the rate of one's slowing down, which is annoying; one's circle of friends unavoidably shrinks, which is depressing; one's body on occasion lets one down, which is frustrating (clambering into a London taxi is a penance); and one's memory deserts one just when it is needed, which is humiliating. But then there can be unexpected miracles.

All my life I have suffered from acute short sight, remorselessly worsening. Old age then further compounded it with cataract and I was finally even forbidden to drive. But lo, technology, so abhorrent in many ways to the old, stepped in; a talented young surgeon implanted a new lens in my one good eye, and suddenly the world about me was renewed; colours were brilliant again, I can see to read and write without glasses and in fact I only need these out of doors. That is a major blessing, thanks to old age.

One thing I believe to be vitally important for everyone, and that is to have an occupation, be it voluntary work of some kind or gardening or even collecting bottle tops. Without this, boredom can become overwhelming. In this respect I have also been lucky, acting as Honorary Secretary and Treasurer to a rather specialized international organization called the World Working Group on Birds of Prey. This keeps me busy, occupies my mind and even provides chances of travel (to conferences etc.) and provides a wide range of friends and correspondents.

There are other compensations too. With all passion spent, no longer to be trammelled by thoughts of sex is a relief. Little things that once would have worried or upset one don't really seem to matter so much, and one can be cheerfully unconcerned by dire predictions of global warming or, as some people think, the next Ice Age. Reading the newspapers, one sometimes feels that the world is becoming so progressively horrible that one can view the prospect of leaving it with comparative equanimity.

I have been quite undeservedly lucky throughout an enjoyable life, but one should never count on one's luck continuing to the end, and I don't.

PLUSSES AND MINUSES

I FIND the pluses and minuses of growing old are not as out of balance as a lot of people might lead you to believe. Here's my balance sheet.

CREDIT

I like the increasing irresponsibility of retirement.

I like getting up even later in the morning.

I like seeing my wife Mary's postbag growing larger than mine.

I'm relieved that sexual competition is more or less a distant memory – like a strip-cartoon fantasy.

I like new friends less and old friends more. The quest for new friends inevitably diminishes – like sexual ambition.

I like occasionally getting a better place at dinner parties than I used to. And waiters and hotel receptionists are more 'oily'.

I am increasingly happy to view, and quite often enjoy, the company of my grandchildren without parental responsibility – indeed, without much responsibility at all.

I like having more time to indulge the appetites and foibles of our pugs. I particularly like the undemanding pace of exercising them.

I'm relieved that I hardly have to shop for new clothes.

I like the fact that with age, in comparison with youth, one is less ashamed to bare one's soul and inner thoughts in inverse proportion to one's body (or the presentable parts thereof).

I haven't yet, I think, reached the point of being gratified by being offered a seat in a crowed bus, but feel I might soon be. The occasion has so far not arisen. I did, however, recently witness an old man say to an attractive girl laden with shopping that he was too old to offer her his seat, but she could safely sit on his lap. After a bit, on the jolting bus, she took the offer up – and after a bit he had to confess that things were not as safe as he predicted. He got a round of applause – and she got a seat.

DEBIT

IRRITATIONS

I hate people who mind about some self-inflicted ailments, which under present law are legitimately brought on. The tax from tobacco (I gave up smoking twenty-seven years ago) brings in far more revenue than the medical cost of treating the victims of the addiction. And the same goes for alcohol. So long as those who indulge in these 'bad' habits are not tiresome, violent, smelly or disgusting, they should indulge to their heart's delight – or demise. As Shakespeare noted:

> They say best men are moulded out of faults
> And, for the most, become much better
> For being a little bad.

I hate medical questionnaires, which pry into my private life and life-style. I don't know what a unit of alcohol adds up to – and don't want to know. The only pleasure I get from such questionnaires is the negative answer I can truthfully give to the query about my history of indulging in strong narcotics. A doctor or dentist should easily be able to tell whether he has a drunk, a smoker or a drug-addict on his hands without the need for questionnaires.

I dislike and feel cross about arguably being more crotchety with Mary, who has been a golden wife for forty-six years – a fault I could effortlessly correct, if the petty side of pride didn't get in the way.

I am increasingly concerned, and frequently embarrassed, about loss of instant memory but take comfort in the fact that this is, in varying degrees, an affliction creeping up on many of my ageing friends.

I am bored by the fact that it takes wastefully more time to do a pee – though I'm not sure how I would otherwise employ the time wasted.

PHYSICAL DETERIORATION

This is potentially – or perhaps indeed is – the biggest item on the debit side of the balance sheet. I had blocked arteries in both legs, went into hospital and was operated on. I was rather surprised when I came round to find that part of my aorta had been replaced with something, I was told, resembling a vacuum-cleaner hose which was connected to the life-flow at the top of the legs. It didn't work as far as the legs are concerned. So I can't walk the Downs or up Scottish hills. I'm only grateful that the blockages have gone downwards rather than to my head – so far.

The trouble with the kind of medical problems I have encountered is that you can't work off alcoholic input as you did when sound in limb. This seems a pity, particularly given that one has more time in a semi-sedentary state to indulge.

Now I'd better go and put the cat out…and shut the chickens up.

THEKLA CLARK
IT DOESN'T ALWAYS PAY

LYING, I have been taught, is reprehensible, inexcusable and a series of other derogatory adjectives. I do so agree. Oh well, a white fib occasionally slips out, but I suppose that happens to everyone. One exception has me in its grip, and try as I might (and I admit I could try harder) I have never been able to shake off this one addictive style of a lie. For as long as I remember I have lied about my age. Up or down, no matter – just so it wasn't really mine.

My mother lied about her age, so I guess you might say I come by it honestly. I should have learned that it doesn't always pay. When she died at what I thought was fifty-eight but was in reality sixty-two – the local newspapers gave her age as sixty-five. By then I had been at it too long for the irony to have an effect.

I began early. I fell in love with my riding master when I was ten. He must have been in his twenties. I told him – and anyone who didn't know better – that I was sixteen. He didn't believe me but, importantly, I believed myself. I have never looked back. When Errol Flynn fell in love with me, I was twelve. On our nightly rendezvous I was any age from eighteen to thirty – depending on the scene we were playing out that night. I lied about my age for college entrance exams, and no one ever found out. I disliked college, so I confessed – hoping it would invalidate my enrolment. My teachers and parents only smiled and seemed almost proud of me, which only strengthened my addiction to falsehood. At eleven I was an avid reader of movie magazines with names like *Screen Romances*, *Silver Screen* and *Photoplay*. On the back pages were announcements of contests for adults only. I entered them all and finally won a year's subscription to a pornographic magazine. I became the most sought-after girl in the fifth grade and started a business selling torn-out pages for ten cents or a Milky Way candy bar. Lying about my age gave commercial as well as personal satisfaction.

'How many more years of high school do you have?' a maiden aunt asked me in front of a Harvard student. The humiliation should have stopped me – or at least cautioned me. Too embarrassed to answer, I looked at him and knew, the way one criminal recognizes another, that he was lying too. Instead of saving me, it confirmed me in my bad, bad habits.

By twenty I had begun to subtract: a condition I keep up today. My husband was younger than I – either two or four or six years, depending on the audience. He didn't mind.

The beauty of living in Italy for someone as steeped in falsehood as I am is the quantity of documents one is required to have. I have a *soggiorno* – a document showing that a foreigner can stay in the country; a *residenzia* – the same but from a different office; a *codice fiscale* – showing something about taxes; a *documento di sanita* – health certificate; a driving licence and credit cards. All have different birthdays on them. It doesn't mean I am not growing old. It just means I can't and won't concentrate on it since I'm not sure exactly how old I am.

MAUREEN CLEAVE
THERE ARE ADVANTAGES

I HAVE some useful tips on how to cope with middle age. Stop saying how expensive things are – terribly ageing. If you have rheumatism in your shoulder, say it's tendonitis. Never be photographed in colour: you may come out with a pink face like Bill Clinton's. Don't wear a baseball cap or shorts. Buy a violent yellow or orange plastic case for your spectacles (we spend a year of our lives looking for things, most of this for our spectacles). Keep a magnifying glass near any new cookery books; these are now printed on pale grey paper in pale grey ink, the page numbers cunningly concealed. It's a good idea to live in the country where looking good for one's age is out of place. It also keeps you in touch with the cycle of birth and death and rebirth.

Remember that, if you have grey hair, you are invisible. The young waiter who has been so chatty and charming and for whom you have left a colossal tip won't recognize you if he sees you in the street two minutes later. There are advantages. You can hang around listening to more interesting people at parties because they can't see you. This won't work if there are too many of you. Groups of grey-haired people are objects of ridicule (though not, I understand, in China).

Lady Diana Cooper's advice was: 'Go nap on the wit.' It's a betting term from a card game and means to stake all, but it's not easy to be witty when wits are what you're losing. It's consoling to remember that, for the young, you may have the mild interest of a historical personage.

I'm lucky in that I have slight intimations of immortality, and I have felt what the seventeenth-century poet Henry Vaughan describes as 'bright *shoots* of everlastingness'.

Transcendental meditation, which I have done for some years, is helpful here. There are exciting interior changes: horizons widen, one is more optimistic, little knots of worry – a fear of sleeping in the house alone at night; a fear of death – begin to loosen. Stabs of guilt about the past and resentments against other people have softened. One is surprised by new insights. Then there is bliss, an irrational happiness that floods the system (rarely in my case but enough to be going on with). Here is Nabokov writing about being in the midst of butterflies: 'This is ecstasy and behind the ecstasy there is something else, which is hard to explain. It is like a momentary vacuum into which rushes all that I love. A sense of oneness with sun and stone. A thrill of gratitude to whom it may concern – to the contrapuntal genius of human fate or to tender ghosts humouring a lucky mortal.'

I know – and I wouldn't have when younger – exactly how he felt.

ISABEL COLEGATE

I WAS TRAPPED

A FEW years ago I found myself, for reasons too complicated to relate, part of a control group for the study of age-related memory loss. We were to be submitted to various tests, the results of which were to be compared to those of a group of people who had sought help from doctors because they feared they were losing their memories. Every week for about two years a rather formal young woman would come to my house, accept a cup of coffee, sit down on the sofa and show me a succession of coloured cards. I then had to remember whether the blue had come before the red, or where in the sequence the green had been. Sometimes the cards had pictures on them and sometimes words. Sometimes they were long words, for which definitions were required. Sometimes there were different makes of car; my answers there must have been very encouraging to the anxious headmasters (for they were mostly retired headmasters, we were told, who used to pride themselves on remembering everything and now were daily reduced to tears by *The Times* crossword). The formal young woman, whose name was Janet, never became less formal, even when we got to the stage of going into the kitchen to see whether I could safely boil a kettle. I was probably quite reassuring here too, being thrown into terrible indecision as to what ingredients to include when making a simple salad.

I eventually became less interested in the whole thing, but since I had undertaken to do it for two years, albeit on the strict condition that an excuse would be found to discontinue the interviews should my own memory collapse (I did not want to have my deterioration monitored, especially not by Janet), I was trapped. My interest revived when something wonderful happened to Janet. She arrived one morning transformed. Her hair, hitherto lank, was swept back in a smooth golden chignon, her lightly made-up face glowed with new found goodwill, her clothes were discreetly fashionable, her shoes frankly frivolous.

'You've fallen in love!' I cried.

But no. An aunt had left her some money, and she had thought she should smarten herself up because she was off to Chicago. Chicago? Chicago, it appeared, was the home of the master computer, the one into which all the findings from all the Janets from all over the world would be fed. Well, but you see, she pointed out, there's a fortune in it for whichever drug company can come up with the definitive memory drug. My romantic speculations dashed, I apologized for my nosiness. Old people *are* nosey, I pointed out, especially old women. That's why you have so few headmistresses on your lists.

I don't know that she much appreciated my unsolicited opinion, but I meant it in all seriousness. Curiosity keeps the brain humming and the memory alert. It may have killed the cat, but it does wonders for the old. I wish I could believe that Janet fed that into the master computer.

DIANA COOPER

BY NIGEL RYAN

HER driving career lasted to the age of ninety-two, warranting, some friend thought, a special police dossier. There was the collision near Hyde Park Corner with a parked car she wanted to sue for dangerous driving, and the bollard that refused to get out of the way. There were regular sightings, too, of the battered white mini with determined figure at the wheel advancing along the capital's pavements. And some half a century after Evelyn Waugh had described her, in the person of Mrs Stitch, descending some cellar steps having omitted to get out of her car, she fulfilled his prophecy.

With her octogenarian friend, Violet Wyndham, she was going to see a film when an inconvenient traffic light turned red. Eyewitnesses claim that her car charged an articulated lorry, reversed and charged again – this time down a flight of steps leading to someone's basement. Nobody was hurt. Violet was shocked. Diana was not. 'There were jewels in my pocket (the shattered windscreen). I sent Violet home in an ambulance and just got to the cinema in time.'

Much has been written about Diana's grandness, and it is her due. But nothing illustrates it more tellingly than the infinite pains she would take to perform humble tasks to perfection, whether duties or kindnesses. If you were sick or downhearted she would be round with Doggie, the Chihuahua – 'No. *Not* like a rat! She's a gazelle!' – to cheer and prod and make you laugh.

JILLY COOPER

'SEXAGENARIAN' IS SUCH A BEAUTIFUL WORD – IT COMES AFTER 'SEX' IN THE DICTIONARY

WHEN I was sixty, I was determined to think positively about that rather large milestone. I decided that on the Monday morning I would race up to the post office and squander my first pension on five bottles of sweet sherry.

Then I'd clank merrily into Stroud for a blue rinse and a cheap visit to the dentist, before reeling off on my free bus tokens to hiccup through *101 Dalmatians* on reduced OAP rates.

The following Monday, I'd draw out another £27.86 and do it all over again. I hadn't been so rich since we lived in London, and I blew the family allowance on vodka and paying the gardener.

'Sexagenarian' is such a beautiful word and comes after 'sex' in the dictionary. It was the image that worried me.

It's hard not to be depressed by signs of decrepitude. The gaps between your teeth widen and become a positive retirement home for bits of ham and chicken, unless you floss like mad. Maybe I should write a beauty book for oldies called *Jill on the Floss*. And I'm fed up with the current obsession with short hair. No one nagged Charles II to have a short, fashionable bob; no one puts pressure on spaniels or high court judges.

The secret of old age is not to listen to alarmist claptrap. The most blissful outcome is that my darling husband can no longer pretend that my sulks, when he's been listening to my imperfections, are caused by PMT.

It may not be necessary to have my face lifted either. Beauticians are making such progress with anti-ageing creams that the wrinkle will soon be obsolete. And as we are about to move back and forth in time, my new youthful, wrinkle-free face may shortly whiz past my raddled old countenance going the other way.

I wish I wasn't too terrified to face the pain of having my bottom lifted or the cellulite sucked out of my thighs. I'll just have to go on saggy holidays for the over-sixties.

I was so lucky to have parents who not only loved each other but taught me to love music, reading, animals and the changing seasons, which all stand me in good stead as I grow older.

'Affection, security…a very good dinner,' wrote T. S. Eliot, are what matter in age. So come the spring and the first unsettling, heady wafts of wild garlic and dog violets, I must try not to fret that the only pass I've had is my bus pass.

Was the euphoria with which I waltzed around the room in my twenties crying 'He rang, he rang' any more intense than the ecstasy I felt when listening to the BBC Philharmonic playing Shostakovich's Eighth the other night? Or the joy, this afternoon, of watching a huge red sun disappearing into the mist like the brake light of Apollo's chariot, as all the robins in Gloucestershire thrust out their chests and sang like little Pavarottis?

'The years seem to rush by now,' wrote George Eliot, 'and I think of death as a fast approaching end of a journey, double and treble reason for loving as well as working as long as there is day.'

Sixty will not come again. I've probably only got a seventh of my life left to read so many books, to write a decent one, to find happy homes for all the stray dogs in the world and to see a unicorn. I might even stop punning, not that I'm an old age pun-shunner.

What is important is to retain one's curiosity and capacity for wonder. 'Old men should be explorers, Always moving into another intensity.' (T. S. Eliot again.)

My hero is the dying painter Ingres, found at the age of eighty-seven painfully and laboriously copying a portrait by Holbein. When asked what he was doing, he replied: 'I am learning.'

COLIN CREWE
LATE YOUTH

As a guide for how to tackle old age I had my brother Quentin, who started to suffer from muscular dystrophy as a schoolboy. By the time he went to Cambridge he was already facing problems similar to old age. He dealt with these as though they were afflictions to be expected and largely ignored. By the time he was in a wheelchair he was still undaunted. In his fifties he made a circumnavigation of the Sahara. When strapped in, he was as adept as anyone at being in a vehicle and at the day's end could sit in a chair, observing the sunset, asking when supper would be, while others unloaded the van and cooked the meal. But it was undeniably an ordeal for him to be so little in charge of his physical destiny. His patience with African bureaucrats, encountered at every border or entrance and exit to every town, was astonishing. That trip was followed by visiting twenty-three islands in the Caribbean and covering 25,000 miles in South America.

The qualities that sustained him were a lively curiosity, an intellectual interest in almost everything, a remarkable lack of self-pity and, above all, great courage.

All this is comparable to old age generally. Many of my generation no longer feel an urge to explore. It is, of course, easy enough in old age to find discouraging reasons not to. These, ideally, should be outweighed by curiosity.

The rejection of new ideas, a classic condition of old age, is personified by a frequent aversion to the computer ('I cannot see the point in having one unless you have a professional need of it.'), resulting in missing out on the modern world.

The rejection of new approaches to life is forgetting things once thought to be impossibly cranky: yoga, therapy and passive resistance, marching against War.

Allow yourself to be as old as you feel. I remember, thirty years ago, being stunned to hear that a man of eighty was skiing at Courchevel. This year, at the same age, I went to the same resort. My skiing was not what it used to be, but it was worth doing. Attitude has changed with a longer span of life. The medieval man at thirty-five was probably making his funeral arrangements.

Above all, it is a pain to refer to one's age when with younger folk. In my youth there was a tiresome observation made by elders when recalling some incident 'years before you were born or thought of...' Irritating and patronizing: implying that you have managed to be born in the un-smart era.

When you meet an ancient person who follows the right rules it is easy to forget their age, in spite of their physical appearance. I remember a group gathering to play tennis and asking Quentin to make the fourth.

Quentin's example has been a great help, but I know many others who are keeping hold of their youth by assuming that old age doesn't have to take over their life that much.

Polly Devlin

God, I'm Glad I'm The Age I Am Now

NOTHING has changed so much in our age as our age. We don't look like older people used to. I think I notice it more than anyone because my shortish life has by chance spanned a conflation of centuries. I grew up in Ireland in the tail end of a dispensation which had lasted millennia and which disappeared in the thirty years between 1925 and 1955. The Second World War was raging but I witnessed the death throes of the oldest kind of social security and the beginning of a new one and spent my youth in a left-over place operating on a timescale of its own, with a way of life that was still affiliated to the earth, nourishing it and being nourished by it, like the fleece on a sheep. Everything was slow, and a lot of the time we lived in the dark metaphorically and physically speaking. There was no electric light for a start, no cars, no instant messaging of any kind, except bolts from the blue from a savage God. It was a last exhalation.

Most people in the district looked old before their time, old women especially. They were monolithic, like henges, had wrinkles like crevasses and bad or false teeth and (hold on, here) wore shawls over black blousy things tucked into gathered skirts that fell to their feet. It maddens me when I see women in films all gussied up in period costume with perky peek-a-boo breasts. No way. Women either had comforting bolsters lying across the tops of their stomachs – waists had vanished long before – or like Crazy Jane's in Yeats's poem: 'Those breasts are flat fallen now'. In any case, if any of us children had ever spied a naked one, we would have died with the shame of it. These women seemed to us unreachably old, yet I know now they were only in their forties, fifties or sixties. I am their age now, yet when I look at photographs of them they are still as old. We, this new late youth generation, don't look like this anymore; and *they* never ever looked as we do now. We should count ourselves blessed. My ageing process (I can't think that I ever came of age as that implies reaching some sort of marker that says 'you're there now', and that has still not happened to me) has been marked by seminal moments, epiphanies really, which pivoted me into different ways of dealing with the new age I found – to my astonishment each time – I somehow had actually become.

The first epiphany occurred when the niece of one of those old women came back from a visit from America. Such a thing was unheard of; everybody knew that when a person emigrated to the States they emigrated for ever. The history of my district was predicated on that loss. Her mother had gone thirty years before to New Jersey and had evidently prospered since here was the returned rich evidence walking to Mass. Seeing the two females together – the venerable *beldame* with white hair piled high in a circular nest, voluminous black bombazine skirts just clearing the ground, her bosom resting on her stomach, her homemade frame shoes giving her walk a characteristic step, and her niece, in a permanently pleated skirt, wedge-heeled shoes, pink short-sleeved blouse, her twin breasts poised for take-off, hair permed and mouth gleaming with Love That Pink – was to witness the collision of two epochs. We were enthralled, as if seeing a bird of paradise for the first time. Her aunt was mortified. But then, her aunt looked like her great-great-aunt, straight out of the pages of George Eliot, and the niece could have stepped out from *The Catcher in the Rye*.

So although that American cutie-pie's looks and style were literally beyond our reach, simply not possible – the local draper didn't do any style other than dowdy – I knew for the first time which age I was going to belong to. I had a template. Between the medieval woman and the American beauty were women like my mother who, though they wore more ordinary clothes – heavy tweed clothes, hats, gloves – moved slowly and were always busy. They had no time to themselves and few beauty aids.

My mother, the most sophisticated woman in the district, used only the faintest trace of Coty lipstick and Goya perfume and Pond's Vanishing Cream. No one exercised, though they worked non-stop, and they ate nothing but carbs and fat: the words 'lithe' and 'limber' weren't in it.

Incidentally, I thought that I was singular in having witnessed the transformation of women from the Middle Ages to glamorous late youth, but I fancy Nancy Mitford was there first. In her marvellous book, *Love in a Cold Climate*, Lady Montdore, that sublime and grotesque creation, is transformed by Cedric from the Easter Island statue she resembles to a little jewelled creature: 'her movements, formerly so ponderous, became smart, spry and bird-like, she never sat now with her two legs planted on the ground, but threw one over the other, which, daily massaged and steamed, gradually lost their flesh and became little more than bone. Her face was lifted, plucked and trimmed…and she learnt to flash a smile brilliant as Cedric's own.'

I mentioned the dame's walk. One of the secret transforming things between us and the people we have left behind – and again, which I saw – is that they moved and walked differently. W. H. Auden, as usual, summed it up brilliantly: 'no unearned income can buy us back the gait and gestures to manage a baroque staircase, or the art of believing that footmen don't hear human speech.'

And I think I am more removed, with my jeans and my sun salutations and downward dogs, from the generation I grew up in, as they were from the Romans.

I spit on Botox and plastic surgery and think them morally untenable, but when I think what else I am privy to now to keep me looking good, what I can buy instantly, I could weep with gratitude. Great dentists, therapies of every kind, yoga sessions, miracle serums – never mind gleaming machines to do the drudgery: most people take such miracles for granted. I, who saw what it was like before, don't think how envious the generations before us would be to know how we have entered our late youth. (I should rephrase that – otherwise it puts me in mind of Peter Ackroyd's imaginative dialogue concerning Oscar Wilde: 'How are you, dear Oscar?' 'I am perfectly well, my dear, thank you. At the moment I am writing a most imaginative account of my youth.' 'I shall send him an invitation also.')

The second epiphany was when Gloria Steinem was being interviewed on her fiftieth birthday, way back in 1984. She was gloriously beautiful: not handsome (as fifty-year-old women were wont to be called then), not fine (ditto): just beautiful. Long blonde hair, smooth skin, lithe body. 'You don't look fifty,' the interviewer said (somehow I hear the word accusing here). 'This is what fifty looks like now,' Gloria replied. I stared at her photograph. Well, I'd met her in the flesh. She was ten years older than me – oh, all right, nine – and she looked ten years younger. I got another template.

I set about myself, became a gym rat, began to break the pattern of ages, the terrible template of middle age towards which somehow I was being rolled by the stones of time, where kitchens is brown, landings is buff, and middle-aged women is square, and Easter Island was my destination.

So many other bonuses. My early youth was spent yearning and fretting and being anxiously restless, in eating too much and then dieting. Youth is so plagued by doubts and despair and the infection of love. My late youth is much happier. The people I love love me. Everything isn't linked to tears. I eat carefully but with pleasure. I don't yearn. Well, not much. On the whole, if I haven't got it by now, I don't want it. That awful emotion of the young – embarrassment – has gone; I actually like exercise. I'm not a gym rat anymore, but I love walking, and I sometimes salute the sun when I see it – so that's not very strenuous. I spend a fortune on creams to make me all smooth and glowing – they don't even begin to work but hey, I feel smooth and glowing underneath.

But the very best thing about my late youth is that, though I look how I want to look and like stepping out with a spring in my step, I know with exquisite relief and great joy that no man will ever look at me again. The relief. Like being unshackled from a lunatic. God, I'm glad I'm the age I am now.

DEBORAH DEVONSHIRE
THE STAGE IN LIFE

I HAVE reached the stage in life when I wake up earlier and earlier in the mornings. The wait till breakfast time has forced me to put a kettle and toaster in my room, so I can help myself to their merciful production whenever I like. I advise all early wakers who have fallen for this plan to buy a clock with a minute and second hand of immediately recognisable lengths, or you may have my disappointing experience of last week. Waking at six a.m., I made and ate my breakfast, only to discover that the clock's similar-looking hands had played a trick on me, and it was in fact only 12.30 a.m. Too early even for me, but too late to pretend I hadn't had breakfast.

LIVING IN THE MOMENT

ENTHUSIASM. That's the trick of staying youthful, flexible, curious and bendable. To achieve this you are forever told: 'It's all in the mind'. What a truism – but how does one keep the mind from dwelling darkly on unpalatable thoughts of growing old, decrepit and worn out? Well, be enthusiastic. Even getting old and dying can be fascinating and, if you are lucky and live to a fine old age, it really can happen. I mean, you die – unlike the failed teenage dreams of becoming a famous and sexy movie star or winning Wimbledon.

Well... Armed with enthusiasm, you can use old age to do things that youth hates – such as giving time to things that do not necessarily get you anywhere. What follows are all sorts of surprises and delights of which you had no notion until the years pressed you into the unimaginable... Like writing this piece.

I am trying to learn how to do things for pure enjoyment. In my youth I was competitive. I remember making my pony miserable, being overwhelmed by a desire to win a potato race. Now I realize that winning did not matter a jot. What mattered was a happy pony and a happy me. I had no luck when I pulled and tugged and gnashed teeth. Now I go slow; love the pricked ears and sensations with no bother about the result.

Every day has become precious. It was not so when I was a teenager. There were long, tedious periods when I did what I did not want to do, not knowing what I *did* want to do. Agonizing self-doubt and silly vanities. Endless passions that blew me 'like deck chairs in a storm' – hopelessly vulnerable – taking up airs and graces because I wanted to make an effect; to impress; to be attractive. Thank goodness most of that idiotic behaviour has gone and now I can be what I want to be, paint pictures with love, enthusiasm and care with a Buddhist acceptance of the result: pleased and thankful if the outside world likes them but equally thankful if that is not the case – as long as I am getting the awareness and pleasure of painting them and a calm acceptance for *what it is*.

I love my spaniel. He is now ninety-five and will soon be a hundred in doggy years. I am fascinated by how he deals with old age. Rabbits and rushing about have passed him by. Now he takes long rests, enjoys the fuss and bother that he causes, likes to be taken out in the car to look at the landscape, is very cheerful and makes the best of everything.

It seems that animals have learned the art of 'living in the moment' to perfection. They concentrate with all their being on doing what they are doing. For the last month I have been observing cows because I have been painting and drawing them. They, like my spaniel, have a busy and contented day. At no moment do they look out of rhythm with themselves or try to live in the past or the future. I am not suggesting that we chew cud or wag tails – but there is a lesson there to learn: whenever possible, live in the moment with concentration and enthusiasm. Now that I am older, I do not have to be competitive or to achieve things: except to achieve things such as delving deeper into painting, loving others and making Clandeboye, my beautiful Irish estate, ever more a source of well being for people to live in the moment. So *hurrah to old age* – it offers such possibilities.

You have to turn it into a friend:

'Look here, old age, now that you have come to stay with me…tell me about all those miserable thoughts that people have about you. All that doom and gloom.'

'I don't think you are right about that,' says old age. 'Can't you see that the past was full of youthful confusion…heaven in a way, but all to do with getting enough, doing enough, achieving enough? Now that I have arrived and plan to stay, see the miracle of life for what it is, and if you are an old human – keep wagging whatever you can and chewing over things with whatever mental faculty that still works. You will be amazed at what happens, not only to you but also to your friends, both young and old. They love a dotty, ancient, enthusiastic relic. It gives them something to aim at.'

Dame Edna Everage
A Reflection On Age

I NEVER think about age, which is probably why I have remained spookily youthful. Sometimes investigative journalists delve into the archives and think they have come up with my birth date, which I have never sought to conceal. They do their sums and express amazement that I am still leaping around on a stage on Broadway singing, dancing and bringing joy to millions. How do you do so much they ask? To which I reply, 'How do you do so little?'

I am a comparatively wealthy woman, though at heart I am still a Melbourne housewife with the same value systems as I had when I was a young wife and mother. Any money I earn goes to my favourite charity, the Friends of the Prostate, or my other good cause, the 'Deviated Septum'. My stage and television work is just for fun, and when you are having fun, you don't age.

Even when I was a young girl I had a few little crow's feet around my eyes, and one day my mother caught me worrying about them in the looking glass. 'They're not crows feet, possum,' she said with her famous wisdom. 'They are the dried up beds of old smiles.' What a lovely observation that was with its subtle reference to the parched Australian outback. I do not go to a gym, but I laugh a lot, which keeps me young and uses muscles we women only use on a few rare other occasions. I have even forced myself to laugh at the misfortunes of others, and that sometimes helps them bear their burden a little more lightly.

I have a wonderful skin, which everyone wants to touch, including strangers, and I don't mind so long as they stay away from my erogenous zones, which, according to a magazine I glimpsed in my dentist's waiting room, seem to be in the most unexpected places these days. I stay young because I pick up the gift of Life and run with it – in heels!

John Fairbairn
Really Rather Agreeable

GETTING older is really rather agreeable, and I have enjoyed each decade more than the one before (although I daresay the first one was pretty exciting, what with the sky being full of German bombers and everybody being pretty nice to one). There are four reasons for the increasing enjoyment. Firstly, people seem to become politer, and one becomes longer in the tooth and growing, easeful deafness protects one from muttered comments like 'boring old fart'. Secondly one stops worrying about what people may think about one's unfashionable garb and banal opinions.

Thirdly, one becomes more observant, paradoxically, as one's eyesight fades, finding more pleasure in the changing seasons and the beauty of buildings which one used to take for granted. And fourthly one's children and their friends – and one's friends' children – become one's friends, and this induces a warm glow.

Lastly, other people's aberrations cease to make one turn a hair, and this is neatly summed up in the following verse narrated to me by my ninety-six-year-old Aunt Margaret:

> The years roll in and the years roll out
> As I totter towards my tomb,
> And I find I care less and less about
> Who goes to bed with whom.

EXCERPT FROM *THE TIME DIARIES* *OF JULIAN FANE*

HERE are a few random rules that should be followed by men: keep yourself clean; get your clothes cleaned as often as possible; do not wear rags; invest in new sober-looking garments; no down-at-heel shoes; do not let your hair grow long; buy a magnifying shaving mirror; only grow a beard in special circumstances and when you can have it properly trimmed; beware dandruff; go to the dentist; never say 'It will see me out' or 'I have bought my last overcoat/air ticket/car'; remain aware of your posture; never stoop or shuffle; never hurry; never drink too much or take drugs that change your personality; try not to complain; do not become a monologist; sympathize with others, if possible; be your age!

A good few of my tips for the older man also apply to women of a certain age, but I would add the following: forget about the passage of time while you remember to exchange your old charms for new ones; yesterday's naughtiness and sulks and pouts will charm no one, and you will have to work harder in order to be popular; steer clear of fashionable clothes; dress to suit your shape; wear trousers with discretion; never even think of shorts; never run anywhere if you can help it; never have a facelift on the cheap; dye your hair, if you must, with caution – you will probably regret it anyway; interest yourself in something other than the opposite sex; retain your femininity, whatever your sexual orientation; laugh at life, however tempting it may be to cry; carry on loving.

The Years Have Rushed By

In the early 1970s, Olda and I came back from London, with two small daughters, to live at Glin. Recently she reminded me of an occasion when I had to show some local antiquarians around one of the great medieval ruined castles of the Fitzgeralds of Desmond not far away from here. A crowd met us in the square beneath the castle wall, and Olda proudly anticipated an admiring audience. Very soon, however, her hopes were dashed as practically everybody boarded the bus for Limerick leaving only a handful of architecture-fanciers to listen to my historical musings!

Olda has not a drop of Irish blood, and her moving to County Limerick was an enormous change for a girl bred in South Kensington. The settling into Ireland was a slow process, and the rescuing and restoration of Glin a considerable challenge. I soon went to work at Christie's, and this necessitated travelling all over Ireland, hunting out things that might be for sale. It also, happily, meant that we bought a terraced Georgian house in Dublin where we entertained clients. It was in Dublin that I was able to write my books on Irish paintings with my old friend Professor Anne Crookshank of Trinity College. Dublin also meant for me the ability to attend committee meetings for conservation bodies such as the Irish Georgian Society, the Castletown Foundation, the Irish Landmark Trust, the Irish Architectural Archive, and most recently as a governor of the National Gallery of Ireland.

Driving the rather dreary road from Glin to Dublin and back, often twice a week, and discovering the highways and byways of Ireland was a combination of excitement and hardship – though traffic in the 1970s and 1980s was not nearly as heavy as today. Now Ireland is congested with trucks, buses and cars, and the infrastructure of our roads and slowly increasing motorways is only just beginning to catch up. Fortunately Dublin can be handled by walking, since traffic there is now a total nightmare. I realize that traffic in most places is pretty dire, but the bus that swept away most of my hoped-for audience is part of a public transport system that is very generously funded by our government. At the age of sixty-six, when we all receive our State pensions, we have the tremendous gift of travelling on public transport – bus and train – free, and this also goes for one's wife, partner, minder or friend! Now I board the train from Limerick station to Dublin and back rather than grappling with the eternal grind of the roads by car. Olda often comes, and the relief and relaxation of reading and working on the train has made an enormous difference to our lives.

Growing older here at Glin has meant more than the humdrum discussion of travel arrangements. One of the greatest pleasures has been the completion of our own residential wing. The main castle is now a small hotel of fifteen bedrooms. Slowly we were being pushed out of our own rooms – sometimes to the loud protestations of our children! The end of our wing was a romantic half-battlemented wood store, and this has been transformed into a beautifully coved new library, more bedrooms and living accommodation. The walls are lined with our books, which are now arranged in logical order and, at the moment, I am writing another book on the history of Irish furniture and interiors from the sixteenth century to 1800. My colleague, James Piell of Christie's is writing this with me, and the pleasure of having a calm and peaceful house to work in, mostly on one floor looking out to the sweeping waters of the River Shannon, is certainly one of the greatest gifts of this period of my life.

The years have rushed by, and the restoring and completion of

Glin is now commemorated by a grey stone plaque inscribed with the dates 1785-2002. One can only hope that we have a few more years together to enjoy it!

GROWING OLD IN GLIN CASTLE

THE garden is full of green doubloons hanging from the branches of the lime trees, and an eerie light sharpens the outlines of the clouds streeling across the estuary. Summer evenings stay light until eleven p.m. and stomping along the gravel paths following the white dot of a ferocious terrier leading the way into the dusk provides a comforting simile for old age. Sight dims and horizons become closer. Ghostly shapes in the crepuscular gloaming indicate the shrubs I know with my inner eye to be there, but the challenge to prune, tidy and tweak them into order is gone. And what a relief!

Options are fewer, and the satisfaction of having shared an enormous part of one's life with one person so that joint interests and the rewards of a long companionship are so many that, smugly, one cannot imagine how people can face a separation and wonder can they realize what they will miss out on in later life? The relaxing familiarity of a loving partnership builds up brick by brick until almost extrasensory fibre-optically refined communication becomes second nature. For the moment anyway it feels like being one half of the same walnut!

To say that I am happy would actually be an understatement, but it was not always thus. Being an English Protestant in Ireland thirty-four years ago was not a popular call, and when I first came I felt like a tooth pulled out by its roots. As Una shut the door so firmly on me as I sat in the smoking room with the coffee cups and pot on a silver tray in 1970 there seemed to be a totally blank canvas ahead. I realize now that all of life is a journey with a clearly defined beginning, middle and end, and how I have got from there to here would be an agony to relate. Battling, confronting, tussling with the past and blindly insisting on the future: suddenly being there and being totally overwhelmed. Clinging and leaning on the unseen, scorned, unfashionable and utterly unconquerable strength of continuity in a country I knew nothing about, I stumbled blindly into bog hole after bog hole. Step by painful step the ground under my feet became firmer and the light at the end of the tunnel brighter. This vulnerable, delicate, extraordinary work of art of which I have become the protector seemed to be encouraging me to take steps that could be fatal: rooms expanded, bathrooms were added, spaces for cupboards appeared from nowhere: it was as if the house was beckoning me to continue. Somewhere to put bottles, somewhere to have a shop; the workshop, the carriage house, and finally the woodshed all lent themselves to a new vibrant positive existence without changing their outward shape. Visitors were lured by every device known to technology, and now they keep coming in a blessed flow to gaze mesmerized at the landscape, explore the ruins of stone-built Norman tower houses, play their games of golf on ancient links high above the western seaboard, take a seaweed bath at Ballybunion, visit the matchless Ring of Kerry, Dingle Peninsular or Cliffs of Moher and to sit in the evenings in the knightly dining room at that most astonishing thing in one's own house: separate tables, while drinking claret and eating my proudest achievement of all: the organic vegetables grown in the walled garden!

The bedrooms are deliciously comfortable and hung with pictures, while you could land a seaplane in the baths they are so big – I feel the astonished gaze of the last twenty-nine recorded Knights of Glin who lived here focusing in on me in utter perplexity. The responsibility is great, but the fun and challenge of it all is enormous.

Young people come and work here in the summers from all over Ireland and indeed, Europe, and our wonderful manager Bob Duff organizes everything while I have all the fun.

Of course doing less takes up more time, but then I fondly imagine that more allowances are made for incompetence. Being a Prod doesn't seem so bad now, and I no longer feel personally responsible for the Irish corpses that hung from the English gallows in vivid Limerick memories. The children are tremendously proud of Glin, and their constant support is the brickwork for my frail confidence. Catherine helps with the garden, Nesta with the shop, and Honor with our publicity; I can feel this great youthful surge of energy coming up behind us. They say they have resolved the problems of feeling English in Ireland and Irish in England and that they are ready to take the place of their ancestors in their country's history. 'Never mind that blather,' I tell them fiercely, 'just remember that each new generation has to put on a new roof.'

When I was engaged to be married I realized that my fiancé truly believed that buildings were more important than people. With the confidence of youth in my immortality I considered this to be heresy and contemplated my forthcoming union with such a stonyhearted individual with considerable doubt. Now that I see how weak and frail and disposable we creatures of water and gristle really are; I realize to my mortification that he could have been right. What greater and more lasting celebration of the human spirit could there possibly be? I have been inspired by this thought for many years now; and with the love that I have come to bear for the lonely place that he brought me to live in and the delight that I take in the miraculous house that we have succeeded in saving and the garden that we are restoring and the beautiful landscape that I look out from every day, I feel well rewarded. When I think of the generations of people's lives that this all represents I am awed by the perseverance of the women and men who lived and worked here and who continue to live and work here. There is always much, much too much to do, and always the changing light on the river and the great wide stretch of open fields on the other side. 'The sun is always shining in Clare,' said Nancy wistfully in 1972 as she drew down the blinds on the sunset.

The lives of all the friends one loves and the things one is interested in are like a continuing story, and one longs to know each week what is going to happen in the next instalment. Inevitably there is going to be an end to the series, but oh I pray not yet.

CHRISTOPHER GIBBS

RIPE FRUIT

WITH the ripening comes certain freedom. The tyranny of daily getting and spending must pass, the gentle dimming of the libido compensated for by the tender sweetness that remains, purged of fear and frenzy. The pace slackens: relish in time all one's own returns with something of childhood's freshness and gleam but without its strictures and anxieties. Waning powers, alien aches and unfamiliar pains come with the luxury of days and nights when, especially if we are single, we may do exactly what we please, providing we have discovered whatever that might be. We can also finally edit out of life all activities (and fellow creatures) that dull delight, releasing a surge of rapture. We laugh a great deal, weep but rarely, wolf vitamins and minerals, slurp flax oil, pick at puddings.

The steady cull of those we have loved (along with those we didn't) seems chiefly to sharpen our affection for the surviving troopers and spurs one to discern in the young the same dear qualities and attributes we've lost. So we seek the gold and the good and finally achieve detachment from the rampaging vulgarity and wrongheadedness that afflicts the fascinating age we live in. We at last have time to follow our noses and less excuse not to.

Blessed in my family and friends and with work that has never bored me, I have not exactly lived a life of privation. Wracked with lust, puffed up with vanity, in thrall to all sorts of nonsense that then seemed glorious, I have lurched along, dodging disaster (more or less), scraping by, occasionally disgraced, but hanging on (again more or less) to the things that really matter: the sense of the divine, 'the signature of all things', Love Divine and all its earthly, earthy echoes, singingly alive in all creation.

Thus I continue work and play long begun, making and shaping a corner of the world that manifests what I've learned so far, a place to call my own and to share with others; now, where Islam and Christendom, Africa and Europe, poor and rich smile across the narrow neck of sea that links the Atlantic and the Mediterranean. I glimpse through the growing town that my beautiful corner is fragile. Am I too? My neighbours include squatters, the moneyed, old and new, the scholarly and the deranged, also many dogs, seagulls and hawks, an owl, bee-eaters (and the bees they eat), a million dragonflies, pretty little snakes and now with its most English of signals, a startled pheasant. There are bright satchelled schoolchildren skipping down the hill to school and fishermen softly talking, as their rods bob above the garden wall. I have a simple house that fits me, a vegetable garden under orange trees, a patch of orchard, a pool, many palm trees, a formal parterre and a green lane that leads to a bit of wild wood and looks down a cliff to the rocky shore and the pounding waves whose sound sometimes fills the trees. I have also the help and support of kind, tolerant, diligent and warm-hearted people, good neighbours and friends who inspire and come and go. Cars are few; planes are fewer. I have a fresh and lovely canvas before me and some years, *inshallah*, to work upon it.

Colin Glenconner
You Can Always Eat The Fries

December 1, 2004, 4.45 pm. Yesterday – my seventy-eighth birthday, as it happens, I was sitting in the front of my car, in Soufrière, waiting for Kent, with my hat well on as usual, and a lady came trailing by, stopped and bent right down to get a good look at me – she said: 'I come and see if age catch you.' As she offered no opinion, I suppose she was satisfied and trailed on.

Here, in St Lucia, age is not a topic to dwell on. Like steak, there are categories. 'Rare', 'medium' and 'well-done'. Having reached the age of indiscretion, I would rate myself 'indigestible'.

But you can always eat the fries.

JONATHAN GUINNESS
TO WHAT DO YOU ATTRIBUTE…?

WELL, I'm still a bit young for the title I have chosen – really one has to be at least a hundred to be asked to what one attributes one's longevity; but I read such interviews avidly. The best ones are those that say a large gin and tonic every day with an untipped Senior Service. Certainly we seem to be less unlikely to make our ton than was the case in the past; a few years ago the Palace, realizing that the Queen was having to send four times as many greetings telegrams as earlier in her reign, began writing to prospective centenarians asking if they really wanted their congratulations. A friend of mine in Ireland was a hundred last year and not only got congratulations from the Queen but also from the Irish President, who unlike the Queen *added a juicy cheque.* There now: hint, hint.

As I said, I am not really that close: I still had to pay for my TV licence this year though for the last time.

Two images spring to mind about getting older. One is that one is sculling down a river with locks, say the Thames, all seeming as level as a lake until one goes through these gates which then shut behind one, and the water goes down. Then lower gates open, and one starts on a new stretch. The lock is what the French call a *coup de vieux.*

The other picture is that one is walking down the spine of an immense armadillo. Any moment one may slip off the side and fall into senility or death. If one is lucky or clever – or does whatever one attributes one's survival to – one manages to stick to the spine. But even the spine inevitably ends at the floor.

What has kept me in shape so far is something so colour-supplement-health-section that I hardly dare admit it: about forty minutes' yoga *every day*. I have been doing it for nearly twenty-five years, ever since a bearded man in an orange robe at the Festival of Mind, Body and Spirit in 1979 handed me a voucher for a free lesson at the Sivananda Centre near Regents Park. Now its address is 51 Felsham Road, London SW15 1AZ, telephone 020 8790 0160 – and no, I don't take a percentage. I've tried two other systems since, but that's the one. They do a beginner's course, which lasts a fortnight, if I remember rightly. Every morning I get up feeling stiff and doddery, do my yoga, then the calendar goes back to – well, middle age. No miracles. It can be unpleasant if one is not feeling well and perhaps some poses have to be given a miss. Every day, please note, and best do it first thing then you will know you have done it. This will mean getting up earlier. You will get used to it.

Watch out, though; your grandchildren will get you to stand on your head and wait for the money to fall out of your pocket.

THE GREAT THING

THE great thing about still being alive is that one can readjust arrangements for one's funeral whenever the urge surfaces.

This activity is a reminder that one is more or less on the move and not completely static as inevitably will be the case when in the horizontal for good. Current instructions for mourners include compulsory smoking, cross-dressing and excessive consuming of Special Brew. Should I predecease my friend George Melly, I would like him to sing 'I'll see you again' in his fruitily modulated impersonation of the Master's Voice.

Selina Hastings
Late Youth

I AM in my sixtieth year but never thought about growing old until a few months ago. I was driving an American couple about London, both slightly older than me, both much face-lifted and intensely age-conscious. It turned out they were shocked by the noise I made when getting out of the car. I would open the door, then with one hand on the back of the seat push myself up. 'Ooooof!' I would go, as I made the not inconsiderable effort. The Americans were appalled. 'Now just stop that!' they cried, exchanging glances of disapproval. 'Stop that noise! It makes you sound so *old*!'

I have stopped the noise. I have also started to take note of other ways in which I might prepare for my senescence: might make it more acceptable both to myself and others. I take more exercise now, not because I enjoy it – I don't – but because it has been borne in on me that with my sedentary way of life I may soon find it difficult to move at all. My mother, who remained extremely fit well into old age, was a great walker and thought nothing of walking from Piccadilly, say, to Primrose Hill when she was in her seventies and early eighties. Now at almost sixty I try to do the equivalent on at least five days out of seven. I'm thrilled, of course, when the weather makes this impossible, but I have to admit I do feel better when I make the effort. Sometimes I even enjoy it, though more often than not I find it loathsome in contemplation and tedious in practice. At those times

I think of the ever-gorgeous Sophia Loren who, when asked in an interview if she didn't find her daily exercise routine boring, replied: 'Boring? Boring? I do not think, Is boring? Is not boring? I just get up and I *do*!'

Two lessons I have learned from older generations are the importance of avoiding self-pity and self-referral. One marvellous woman whom I used to visit fairly regularly made my heart sink by her copious wallowing in self-pity. Trying to distract her, I would begin, 'I saw such a good film last week.' 'Oh, did you?' she would resentfully reply. 'Nobody ever takes *me* to the cinema.' Another made conversation impossible by insisting always on dragging the subject round to herself. 'I see two terrorists have been captured in Afghanistan,' someone says. 'Do you know, *I've* never been to Afghanistan?' she will brightly inform us.

Other than that, I hope to keep working as long as possible, while praying for a wonder drug to boost my failing memory, and I also hope that it will be a few years before I am forced to take seriously the process, not of growing old, but of growing up.

JOHN HAYLOCK

THE PUNISHMENTS AND THE JOYS OF AGEING

THE three main punishments are: the loss of friends, forgetfulness and the deterioration of one's physical powers.

Often one says to oneself: 'Now if only So-And-So were alive, he would enjoy that and we would both laugh, or he would agree about some monstrosity and we would both express our rage.' Names, of course, even of close friends are swallowed by Lethe, and one may have to go through one's entire address book to retrieve one. And the cordless phone, where has it got to?

One gets used to physical disorders. One postpones getting up from an armchair when one needs to look up a word in the dictionary, which is at the other end of the room. One drops a letter and leaves it on the floor, as picking it up requires a painful effort. One can't hear what people say, especially the gabble of a caller who rings up and tells one something unintelligible. Walking is a problem, even with a stick, and getting into a bus or a London taxi involves a struggle. Hurrying is nigh impossible, above all when one should be as quick as at the checkout in a supermarket; one fumbles for the right change, to the irritation of impatient shoppers in the queue. When stationary at a traffic light the driver of the car behind hoots if one doesn't storm ahead immediately it turns green.

The joys mitigate the punishments. It is a joy not having a job one has to go out to perform. Taking one's time to do simple things like getting out of bed, making breakfast, having a shower and dressing. It doesn't matter how long one takes. One can enjoy the interruptions like the arrival of the newspaper and then the mail; both provide excuses to pause in the proceedings of preparing oneself for the day. Postponement is another joy. 'Oh, I can do that tomorrow,' one tells oneself, and when the morrow comes one has forgotten what one was supposed to do. One can read what one wants to – not what one has to. The greatest joy is being alive.

DRUE HEINZ
HOW DOES IT FEEL TO BE OVER FIFTY?

HOW does it feel to be over fifty? Cannot remember.

Missing presumed dead…

Desirability – for one. Desirability – for you. Desirability – for the world.

Blessing was great
Withering was annoying
Waiting is worse.

MIN HOGG

GROWING OLD GRACEFULLY OR NOT

I AM in a continuous muddle about getting old. Am I seventeen or sixty-six? I'm blessed if I know. One minute a grandmother knowing how to suck eggs: the next, begging for a mentor of five or twenty-five to teach me how to run my life online. I have discovered falling in love with somebody smooth (as opposed to somebody wrinkly) every bit as rewarding and wretched as it was half a century ago, but at least age has taught me to keep a spare compartment somewhere in my brain, a sort of packed suitcase ready for the quick getaway.

I don't feel inclined to take a nap in the afternoons, but nor am I pleased to stay up all night dancing my socks off. Occasionally, spending the whole evening at home by myself, a whole bottle of wine will disappear, but I get less squiffy with it now, and I still smoke like a chimney – especially, like today when I have some writing to do, puff, puff, four fags since starting this.

Exercise, which I never, ever, used to do, I take in the form of swimming once or twice a week in a public pool, a quarter of a mile each time. It has done wonders for my smoker's lungs.

I don't much like what I see when, with my long-distance specs on, I come upon myself in an unexpected mirror, yet when I am with young people I feel inside exactly the same age as they are and am madly grateful the generations mix together so effortlessly.

It has taken a while adjusting to not going to an office anymore, I miss the hubbub, the running jokes and the adrenalin of a brilliant idea emerging, but how divine it is these days to concentrate on one piece of work instead of juggling with hundreds of simultaneous problems as I used to, not to mention the bliss of travelling whenever I choose.

I do wish fashion would take a turn for the better though, that really was nicer in the past. Why do girls insist on dressing up like tarts and then be all huffy when they are groped at the photocopier? I like to dress quite jauntily, but the places where I can find such things have dwindled to well nigh zilch. Luckily I do have a whole room full of clothes so shall have to make do and thank my lucky stars I can still get into thirty-year-old things.

I am not looking forward to decrepitude, but I come from long-life stock; my mum was doing the Hokey Cokey aged 101 – in spite of two hip replacements, so I guess there is hope I won't crumble too radically.

HUGH HONOUR
LOOKING FORWARD

LOOKING forward keeps me going. I clutch at the unconquerable hope that the book on which I am working will be better, at least more satisfying to me, than anything I have previously written and allow me time to begin another long meditated project. I look forward to the arrival of old and new books I have ordered and of periodicals – including the *Weekly Guardian*, which invites readers to give subscriptions to friends and 'share the good news' although no paper makes a greater speciality of bad news. Out of doors, the expectation that plants in the little jungle that surrounds me will continue to overgrow dispels the sadness of changing seasons.

Although I had a happy childhood, my main ambition was to grow up. When taken to a performance of *Peter Pan* I was utterly mystified, as many other normal children must have been. I wanted to be allowed to stay up late. Soon I was asking for long trousers, conceded if only as armour against paedophiles. (Old men who wear shorts and unwittingly make themselves look still older merit a psychological study.) Shaving was another fulfilled ambition still enjoyed as a morning ritual. And then driving the car: taking charge of a lethal weapon, as my mother warned me. 'Youth's a stuff will not endure' – and a good thing too, I began to think. The youthful appearance I retained was a handicap when I began to write reviews of art exhibitions for *The Times* as 'a correspondent', 'a special correspondent' finally 'our special correspondent' but without a name. Functionaries eyed me suspiciously as the representative of a paper that was still internationally respected. I longed for grey hairs, if not quite as many as I have today.

For fifty years I lived and worked with a companion who was perceived to be older than I was, though the age gap of no more than eight years became decreasingly significant and seemed almost to close. At home, he was addressed as 'Signor Fleming', and I, as I still am, '*Signorino*' ('master' – in the English usage of my childhood). In my professional world, however, I am treated with the deference accorded to age in Italy and have difficulty in persuading young colleagues to address me familiarly and by my Christian name as 'one of the boys', although I do not dye my hair or wear short trousers.

Never celebrating my birthday, I thought little about how old I was until quite recently when deteriorating eyesight made me acutely aware of advancing age, and an operation for cataract was recommended. 'Don't have it,' Viviana shrieked across a dinner table, 'It's a terrible *shockkk*.' I did, and it was. When I took off the bandage next morning, the lined, grazed and haggard face that scowled back at me from the mirror was at least twenty years older than I had supposed it to be. As I went through the house, I saw cracks in the walls, scratches on the window panes, stains on upholstery, tarnish on the silver but also colours brighter than I had ever registered and in works of art, exquisite details that I had forgotten. Everyone I met seemed to have put on twenty years since the previous day. So I wonder whether I am not seeing myself as others see me, or whether they continue to see me as indistinctly as I had previously seen them. I overheard someone say of me: 'he's seventy-seven but doesn't look a day over sixty-nine.' Apparently I do not yet pass muster to attract gerontophiles – but there is still hope for the future.

Elizabeth Jane Howard
A Classic Slipstream Situation

GETTING old is a classic slipstream situation. It's rather like that game Grandmother's Footsteps. I stand at the end of a lawn with my back to a row of the trappings of old age whose object is to reach me before I turn round and send them back to their row. One or two of these have caught me out during the last five years; I have neither the health nor the energy that once I had. In these respects I am not as young as I feel. Arthritis is dispiriting because it's both painful and incurable, and it takes time to become reconciled to it. I can't – like my friend, Penelope Lively – garden anymore, and that is for both of us a privation.

But on the plus side, I am able to go on writing, I can sew and cook and have friends to stay and above all read. I continue to go to my women's group; I can still learn. One of the good things about living longer is that we have more time to learn *how* to be old. It's clear to me now that inside the conspiracy of silence about age – because of the negative aspects of the condition – there is the possibility of art: that is to say that it can be made into something worth trying to do well, a challenge, an adventure. I don't want to live with any sort of retirement, with nostalgia and regret wrapped round me like a wet blanket. I want to live enquiringly, with curiosity and interest for the rest of my life.

113

WALKING DOWN THE AVENUE

UNFASHIONABLY, I'm not at all keen on old age. All the things that oldies used so boringly to whinge about in my youth are coming to pass: stiff joints, loss of glasses twenty times a day, trouble opening the front door, wine causing a headache rather than merriment. Then there's the total incomprehension regarding the mysteries of communication that seem to have taken over the whole world, and the melancholy caused by never being able to speak to anyone because they're either checking their emails or on their mobile telephones. There's the fury at what's happening to our language, in the Church of England and elsewhere… And as for *looks*: the knowing one will never, ever look better again. Ah, vanity. I won't go on.

But I don't often think of those things, and many more, because I don't have the time. Oddly, I'm busier than I can ever remember in forty-seven years of working life. This is partly because I can never say no to even the smallest request. Would you contribute a recipe with a funny story attached for my cookbook? Yes, yes. Would you drive four hundred miles to a small arts centre to talk to the dozen people who just might brave the rain? Of course. Would you give away our prizes and make a twenty-minute speech giving advice on entering the grown-up world? Why on earth not?

Accepting such requests makes the isolation needed for the more serious work of writing ever harder to find. But spurred – thank goodness – by constant ideas, I do somehow manage to stick to an old discipline – write from 8.45 till 1.30 – which I love. I stick to it even on holiday: thus, with a ridiculously puritanical sense of well being, I 'earn' the free afternoon. Recently I've been working on a novel in the mornings and compiling an anthology in the afternoons: 150 hand-written letters requesting contributions, followed by reminders to these equally busy people who forget to send them. This doesn't leave much time or, sometimes, energy for visiting the ninety-four-year old mother, the married daughter and three grandsons in London and trying to be motherly to the undergraduate daughter and her myriad friends who need a lot of feeding and sympathy at exam time. Then there's the twice-weekly imperative at Sainsbury's, the planting of four hundred tulips, the general smooth running of a largish house. There are the trips all over the place to hunt down old paste jewellery for my next sale. All recognisable stuff in a pretty average life. Rather odd, though, that that rare thing, *a moment to oneself*, is so much more elusive at sixty-six than it was twenty years ago. Still, I believe that hard work and a busy life is an antidote to ageing. To me retirement is unthinkable.

When I've a moment to read a paper I notice the pleas to take exercise if one wants to ward off heart attacks and the general crumbling of old age. I've thought about this obviously good advice. But when is there time for exercise? I do sometimes walk through the park. That's pretty boring. And the alternative of rattling flabby flesh in an earnest gym is not for me. But exercise, I told myself two years ago, I must. Then I found the happiest of all answers: tap dancing.

In fact – nothing to do with exercise – to be a tap dancer has always been my fantasy: the top hat, the white tie, tails, cane, the dizzying click of the shiny shoes – Fred Astaire, Gene Kelly, me. For a sublime ninety seconds, in 1967, I did a routine (it took six weeks to learn) with Cleo Laine on television. It was the occasion of some William Walton anniversary on an arts programme that I used to present. I had taken my chance to make the bold suggestion to Cleo: wouldn't it be best if she and I did it together?

It was live TV. The recording, sadly, was dumped by the BBC, so I only have two faded photographs as proof of my star turn. It was terrifying. It was bliss. And having relived the moment for over thirty years, the thought suddenly occurred: it's time to make a comeback.

I found a wonderful teacher, Karen. She is a brilliant natural dancer. One day, still in her job as a paramedic, she watched that enchanting film *Stepping Out*. I could do that, she said to herself. And she could. In a trice she had risen from pupil to inspiring teacher.

Her classes take place in a heart-sinking, disinfectant-smelling hall in Cowley. In my class I'm the oldest by about three decades, but it doesn't seem to matter. I was apprehensive at first, but once my ball-change returned (you never quite forget, like riding a bicycle) courage and enthusiasm soared. Now, after almost two years, I'm getting there. By that I mean I'm being pressed to take my Bronze Medal. To date I've resisted, although I do rather fancy a Bronze Medal in tap to add to the few books on my CV. Impatient to progress with all possible speed, I also have a private lesson every week. In an old workingman's club, every Wednesday afternoon, Karen and I have almost perfected 'We're A Couple Of Swells' from *Easter Parade*. It's a long routine – four minutes – and the problem is more in remembering what comes next (Ginkgo Biloba is absolutely no help to tap routines) rather than accomplishing the steps. We have the top hats, the canes: the full gear. Soon we're to perform it at a charity show, when I hope no one will ever guess how long it's taken to learn.

So tap dancing is far more than exercise: it's the most reviving and delightful two hours of my week, the essential escape from the daily hum of an overcrowded life. I love the feeling of serious achievement when suddenly I master a tricky step – that wonderful moment when the impossible becomes the possible. I would not put off my weekly sessions for anything. No, not for the merriest party in London. Because in a frenetic elderly life you need your private moments of challenge to keep you mentally and physically spry. So for me 'Walking Down The Avenue' every Wednesday afternoon, swinging my cane in Cowley is the answer, and I hope to remain a happy old hoofer for many years to come.

MUCH MORE FUN

I WAS born in 1940 and, looking back, the last fifteen years have certainly been the best of my life. The younger me wanted so much to be engaging, helpful and good. Now I am less anxious to please or to be good. And it is much more fun.

In 1993, after eight re-singled years, I remarried. My husband is a historian. We skip about when our grown-up children aren't watching. We visit pubs, churches, museums and walk over the Cotswold hills with backpacks filled with sandwiches and plastic macs. We laugh a lot, particularly about the ageing process. Over candle-lit dinners it is not of love we speak, but of meat that gets stuck in our teeth and my inability to drink almost anything without getting tipsy, or of the pains that strike the neck, feet or whatever.

My sister frequently says I am a 'course groupie', and it's true. I have always been hungry for knowledge. Two years ago, at a history course, I developed a passion for Elizabeth I's England, which led to enjoying sixteenth-century music and poetry.

I love listening to Radio 4. I told my husband when I married him that, if I left him, it would be for the radio. I have gleaned information from all over the world, of what people can do with their lives and what they think about. I can imagine all this while scurrying about domestic duties.

I keep a card by my desk with a picture on it of George Eliot. The quote underneath says: 'It is never too late to be what you might have been.' Last year, armed with this idea and desiring for many years to write poetry myself, I went to a poetry workshop week in Devon. It was hard work and a bit frightening but an enlightening experience, and as a result I joined a poetry creative writing class in Oxford. In it there are several ex-academics who write obscure lines littered with Greek mythology, about which I know nothing. But – and this is the point – I have had three poems of a more ordinary nature published and have received £6.00 in payment. J. K. Rowling, with her Harry Potter success and millions, could not have had more pleasure than I have had with mine and the £6.00 in coins I received, secure in a plastic bag.

Last year, reluctantly, I joined a 'senior movement' class, thinking that the exercise would do me good. It was not a success. I cannot tell left from right in an instant, and instructions were lost on me. I simply could not follow and gave up. But I am fortunate in living in an extremely pretty, small market town and find the exercise I enjoy in walking round it.

And I like ironing, going to church, dancing in the kitchen to old Beatles records and making apple crumble. I love playing with my grandchildren and admit I am a contented oldie, enjoying small pleasures and experiencing new freedoms.

CHARLES KEEN

THE CHATTERING CLASS

No sound of tiny footsteps pattering,
No office to attend;
A life of reading, rambling, chattering
With family or friend;
We may not find the mirror flattering,
But why should we pretend?
We wag our tongues, our minds we stand at ease:
Such is the laid back life of OAPs.

A book of verses 'neath the bough,
As sang the bard of old,
A jug of wine to smooth the brow
And keep away the cold.
Hang up the briefcase, park the plough;
The vesper bell has tolled.
So light the evening lamp, uncork the booze,
Plump up the cushions for a fireside snooze.

We may need hearing aids to hear,
We may need specs to see;
But what we *think* we heard we cheer
With glad, convivial glee.
Though lame, we do not shed a tear,
But glow with bonhomie.
We walk the dog, we cultivate the garden,
Actively pottering, lest the arteries harden.

Some, too, have physical facility
To dance, to swim, to hunt,
Cutting their capers in tranquillity,
Leading from way in front.
Others play croquet with agility
And scarcely a puff or grunt.
Light-heartedly we wear our Annos Domini,
And damn the discontented to ignominy.

Up with the older generation!
Up with the wrinkly crowd!
Age is a cause for celebration,
Something to make us proud,
A *hopefully ongoing situation*,
The lining within the cloud.
So long as we've abundant wine and chatter,
We really feel there isn't much the matter.

Mary Keen
Selfish Granny Syndrome

AFTER turning a somersault for the first grandson, I cricked my neck for a year and I know I will never vault a gate again. Pushing wheelbarrows up hills feels more virtuous than thrilling – and dancing in public is inclined to scare the next generation. For an overweight speed junkie, the sea is the answer. In water it is easy to feel thirty and bursting out of my skin with energy.

About North Cornwall every summer I dream all year. Not Rock, full of Sloanes, but the wild coast further north, where sand stretches for miles and nobody smart goes. Ever. The caravan park puts them off and the rocks are wet and mussel crusted, which is hopeless for reading or sunning. The sand never dries enough to put a towel down and picnics are gritty, unless we take to the pebbles, where wasps arrive from the cliffs. The point of the place is to find an empty stretch of sea so that we can spread ourselves down the beach, in a line of family boards, all catching the same wave. To do this, we have to walk a long way beyond the lifeguard's zone, where the water between the flags is thick with colliding swimmers. At low tide, the body boards can bump along behind grownups, while children try to sneak a ride for buckets and spades that they are bored of carrying and dogs threaten to drink seawater, which everyone knows makes them mad. Before the perfect place is reached on a receding tide, there are always a few rocks to navigate and some scary deep pools to wade through. Once there, we pitch a small orange tent for anyone under two, because it is usually windy and often it rains. The sea is always the warmest place. You need to get into it fast.

When the sun shines it is the best holiday ever. You can spend eight hours on the beach wearing a bathing suit with no danger of feeling embarrassed by the body police. (There are plenty of subjects for Beryl Cook to paint at the start of the long trek to the perfect place.) The grandchildren wear wetsuits, but the grown-ups prefer skin, although the daughters are inclined to be doomy about skin cancer and spend much of their day anointing any parts of their children left uncovered. I have been more sunburnt on a Cornish beach than anywhere else on earth. The only flaw to hot days is Selfish Granny Syndrome. I cannot be on hand to supervise grandchildren in rock pools, or terriers on permanent alert for other dogs and joggers, because I want to be in the sea – with the state-of-the-art body board all the time. Especially in the three hours leading up to high tide, when the waves are really rolling. Luckily, the older grandchildren are as addicted as I am, so I have an excuse to be in the water with them. Husbands are less keen on surfing, and when they volunteer for dogs and rock-pool duty, the daughters can come in too and we all try to catch the same wave. 'Not this one…not this one, but the *next*,' we yell and if we are lucky, we are all on it, creaming in with the foam and shouting to each other above the rush of water. It is tempting to sweep in as far as you can, but walking out to the next wave can be heavy going, so I bale out before the shallows and head out to sea again. On the way back we argue about whether paddling helps you catch the wave and how putting the nose of the board down can make you go faster, although if the tip goes too far under, you risk an underwater somersault.

The ideal moment to jump on the board is as the wave curls over to break and plenty of them are scarily higher than my head and twice as high as the children. Unless you are prepared to dive through the breaker, which I am not, there is no way out but to go with the water.

The sense of danger is all part of the excitement. When the huge ones come, we shout: 'I'm scared. I'm scared.' On a good day I spend about five hours in the sea. Two hours is not too long to stay in for one session, waiting for just one more perfect wave, and it is usually guilt, rather than cold, which gets me out. If we get really cold, there is hot chocolate, or someone treks back to the café for coffees. At the end of the day we have to climb the secret path up the cliffs, carrying wet bathing suits and surfboards and walk over the top to get back to the car. Next morning I am so stiff and tired, I can hardly get down the stairs at the rented cottage, but as soon as I am back in the sea, I feel ready for anything again.

LINDA KELLY

SO FAR, SO GOOD

I THINK what I miss most about being young are the clothes – and the figure to wear them. The other day I was in St Tropez, and saw a deliciously slinky, shocking-pink satin suit in a shop window. I looked at it with a pang of longing, thinking sadly: 'If only I were forty years younger!'

No more shocking-pink satin, alas, but there are compensations for being old. It's good to have survived this far – sixty-eight years of experience banked – and nothing can take away the pleasures they've included. There's a comforting feeling of solidarity with friends, and even acquaintances, of the same generation. We've all lived through the stretch of time; even though we've been pursuing our individual destinies, we've all been part of the same zeitgeist. And old friendships, like good wine, get better and better – though I hope I go on making new ones too.

What are the other things that I appreciate about having arrived at this stage of life? I don't suffer agonies of embarrassment anymore; I suppose I've put my foot in it so many times by now that one mistake more or less no longer seems to matter so much. Then there's the books I'll never have to read again. I've been through *Ulysses* once and that will have to do. Others, like *Finnegans Wake*, I'll never get round to at all. With only a limited span ahead, it's time to return to old favourites: Jane Austen, Dickens, P. G. Wodehouse and, my equivalent of Valium, detective stories. And it's always exciting to come across a good new young writer and to feel that civilization carries on.

Family life is so precious that it almost seems bad luck to write about it. But I could never have anticipated the joy of being a grandmother – the enthusiastic hug of greeting, the small hand slipped into one's own. Or the cosiness of having been married for over forty years and the fun of sharing things together. There are moments like today, walking in the woods on a lovely autumn afternoon, when all one can say is '*O temps, suspends ton vol.*'

It won't, of course, and who knows what lies round the corner? All one can do is think of Philip Larkin's poem 'The Mower' – 'We should be careful of each other, We should be kind while there is still time' – and bash on as best one can.

LATE YOUTH

WHEN my mother died at the age of 102, it was not from cancer, heart failure, diabetes, stroke or Alzheimer's but from a disease far more insidious and common. She died of boredom. 'Oh, I'm so *bored*!' was her constant complaint when I visited her. Her sight was so poor that she could no longer watch television or read a book even in outsize print. She was so deaf that she could hardly hear the wireless or what her visitors were shouting at her. Eventually 'Oh, I'm so *bored*!' was one day followed by 'Can't you ask the doctor to give me an injection?' I replied that no, I was afraid that I couldn't do that – and that he couldn't do that. 'Well, call the vet, then!' she snapped.

All my life, I too have been the victim of the same disease. It is commonly believed that the pursuit of happiness – whether achieved through ambition fulfilled or love reciprocated – is the dominant human motive. But I do not share that belief. For me the dominant emotion has always been the avoidance of boredom; and, though they might be unwilling to acknowledge it or may even be totally unaware of it, I think that the same is true of many other people. When individuals shoplift, though far from being overdrawn at their banks, commit adultery, though far from being dissatisfied with their marriages, indulge in dangerous sports for which they have no aptitude, recklessly throw up lucrative jobs or smoke, inject or sniff drugs, it is all too often, I am convinced, out of desire to escape the terrible *ordinariness* of their existences. In my own case, whenever life has seemed too regular and safe, I have introduced some element of risk into it. My attitude has always been: Down with rest cures, up with unrest cures!

The fact that, because I was as improvident as any actor, pop star or professional footballer during my good (i.e. profitable) years, now I have to continue to work into my ninth decade in order to be able to pay the ever-increasing rent on my house, I sometimes of course regard as a curse. But far more often I regard it as a blessing. I see so many of my previously busy contemporaries dying of boredom as they go on expensive cruises, spend the day on the golf course or pass the afternoon in a half-empty cinema watching trivial films at concessionary prices. The other day an elderly neighbour, once a frenziedly busy financier, stopped me in the street: 'Where are you rushing to?' he asked. 'I'm late with a review. I must catch the last post.' 'Oh, how I envy you!' he said. Better to be obliged to rush through life than to be reduced, as he now was, to ambling through it.

The other thing that I am convinced keeps me active, energetic and, yes, alive is the insatiable curiosity that I have had since my earliest years. Many years ago I was marooned in Salonika in the winter, in the immediate aftermath of the Greek Civil War. The electric supply, which came not from a power station wrecked in the war but from a cruiser moored in the harbour, constantly failed; there was no adequate heating in my flat; when it did rain, it sleeted, and when it did not sleet, it snowed. I sank into what I now realize was a clinical depression. Each morning I awoke, saying to myself: 'If things haven't improved by tomorrow, I'll kill myself.' That I did not do so was because each day I wanted to see what the next one would bring. Would the heavily pregnant wife of a colleague of mine have a boy or a girl? Would my maid at last pluck up courage to leave the husband who constantly beat her? Would a Greek footballer friend be selected for the local team? Today, to a large extent, I am similarly kept alive merely by the recurrent questions: What on earth is all this about? What the hell is going to happen next?

I can recommend these two things – the avoidance of boredom and an insatiable curiosity – as far more effective antidotes to the inroads of old age than any pills, plastic surgery, physiotherapy, diets, vitamin supplements or visits to the gym.

A DIFFERENT PERSPECTIVE

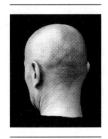

I'VE just bought my first motorcycle. It's very exciting to find a new freedom.

I'm half-Thai and part Dutch-Javanese but made the brilliant decision to live and work in Italy. Tuscan storms are thrilling. Far better than the Dutch ones. As a child, in Holland, I loved thunder, lightning and heavy rain. In later youth, with the development of self-consciousness, storms represented something inhibiting and inconvenient – wet clothes, soggy shoes, arriving at parties looking half-drowned. Now, in middle age, they have become thrilling once again. The world has taken on a different perspective. I enjoy everything more and mind everything less. Far less. More philosophical. The luggage I've accumulated helps me to see the world in better perspective. It's helpful to try to look at things through the eyes of a child, to remember how I felt.

I'm having my photograph taken. From the back. More mysterious without a nose or a mouth. Facelifts are ridiculous. The face must go on growing until the end. It's crazy to try to go backwards.

I think a lot about death. I think very Asian. I believe in an afterlife but have no idea what it will be like. Sinister and mysterious. Working with my partner, Walter Fabiani, in the antique trade keeps us both young. We sell and buy all over the world. Travel is intoxicating. You never know what will turn up. This year we bumped into Susanna Johnston at the Inlay Lake, Burma.

I'm health conscious and go to the gym most days. I do that entirely for myself – to keep flexible. Nothing to do with how I look. When I go to parties, which I adore, I dress well. This is from a sense of duty to my host. I like to be a part of the general décor. It has nothing to do with the impression I make. Those worries have been cured by the passing of time.

Food presents me with a passport to happiness. Nostalgia for the past can be combined with the present and the future. As a child one was presented with something to eat. Now I remember my favourite dishes and recreate them. My cooking is a mixture of everything. Italian, Thai and Indonesian. I live in an apartment in an ancient palazzo looking out to a medieval piazza where I love to entertain friends.

I like to make Semoor: an Indonesian dish. I skin and bone a chicken – then cook everything very, very slowly; adding Asian spices. Onions and tomatoes. I cook the chicken until it is almost black then add hardboiled eggs. I also add sweet soy sauce, which turns the eggs black and nobody can think what it is they are eating. It puzzles people. For me, this dish is a reflection of childhood: ready to have it again.

When I was fifty I asked for roller blades as a birthday present. They were not invented when I was a child, but I used to love roller-skating. I was ready to skate again – but faster.

LUCINDA LAMBTON
IF THIS IS BEING A FOOL IN PARADISE...

'AGE I do abhor thee, youth I do adore thee' – attributed to Shakespeare in the *Passionate Pilgrim* – are words that positively scrunch my senses with perplexity at how wrong they are. Every stage of life is surely to be relished in equal measure, and unless of course beset by some misfortune due to the galloping years, should be cheered on to the last grateful lap.

Surely the only way to progress along the passage of time is to celebrate it. It would be a sin to do otherwise.

My sixtieth birthday party was a full whack gala with hundreds of pals, some fifty children and as many dogs, all prancing and dancing together to the heart-lifting, toe-tapping tones of a blue grass band.

A giant old-fashioned marquee in the garden was festively attired with flags and bunting and with dozens of 'Medieval' banners from the Palio in Siena. I have had them for years, and they never fail to come in handy! There were hundreds of billowing balloons of every colour, and many with '60' shrieking from their curves. They flew forth everywhere, with nine-foot high bunches swaying at either end of the delectable, teatime-treat-laden table, along with mounds of wild flowers: buttercups, may, cow parsley and marguerites. The company of hundreds sang 'Happy Birthday' four times. How I love that American song composed in 1935, by two Louisville teachers, one of whom – delightful to discover – was professor of education at

Columbia University! To hear it is to be imbued with a sense of affection, to be enfolded by a cloak of cosiness, embraced by friends' voices, instead of by their arms. Almost everyone said how brave it was to proclaim the six decades. One Jamaican pal wrote that she 'ran and hid at Milk River Baths for three days and wouldn't come out'. Three days, no doubt, of wise reflection, as against one of unconsidered, but untrammelled, joy!

I am lucky (or un-thoughtful) enough to have an ever cheerful and optimistic disposition and have never, ever stopped to think of the advancing years as being anything other than life itself. At only sixty-one, I can still crow that I have not noticed any dispiriting changes; if this is being a fool in paradise, then that is exactly what it is. Certainly it is my good fortune to be oddly immune from reality when it suits the bill, and I suppose that ageing must be the top of that bill, every minute of the day. I have been asked to write down what getting old is like, and I can truthfully say that I do not know. Yet!! On and off for the last four years, I have been battling my way through the jungles of Jamaica, discovering vast great Palladian ruins, some unseen by man for over 150 years. At one point I collapsed and was flown home, both to a major operation and to be told that I was near death but instead had blundered on, macheteing my way through life. When the final trumpet blows I would like to go like Queen Victoria, as was written by one of her Indian subjects in 1901: 'Earth to earth, Ashes to ashes, Into the tomb the great Queen crashes.'

KENNETH JAY LANE
THE PRIMARY 'DON'T' BEING 'DON'T DIE'

ONE must be very careful at the approach of maturity – my favourite word for the shadow of senility. Fortunately I've found a few 'do's to guard against the 'don't's. The primary 'don't' being 'don't die'.

In order to guard against the bugs and their cousins the germs, I have found that smoking is the best defence. This is a bit difficult in New York where puffing away is not only unpopular but actually forbidden in public places, including restaurants, bars and even workshops. Many of our leading hostesses have recently developed allergies to secondary smoke, having nothing to do with the fortunes they have spent to learn to stop their most pleasurable habit. They also claim that smoking makes them short of breath, making the climbing of stairs of which they partake four evenings a week more difficult.

Another defence against yet another bug (or several others) I have found reasonably effective but not quite as pleasurable as smoking is sexual abstinence. Here, however, Mother Nature has come to the rescue, slowly turning off the gushing faucet of libido. On the plus side is the extra time one has for reading, watching late-night television films and playing gin rummy. Fortunately, I'm lucky at cards – if not at love. The green-eyed monster no longer lurks.

In closing, I would happily embrace 'maturity' if I could only lift my arm.

TORY LAWRENCE
THROW AWAY THE FROCKS

BUT I can't. They hang, like shot game birds, shoved to the far side of the wardrobe.

At least I'll never have to put them on – never have to go to another of that sort of party and wait around for an invitation to dance.

The doctor said 'Your liver's trying to tell you something' when I complained, thirty years ago, of not being able to consume my usual amount of red wine. So now I never have those huge, helpless hangovers and the terminal embarrassment of wondering who I've insulted or what I've done and to whom the night before.

'Oh, you do look well' means you don't look *too* dreadful nowadays. And occasionally when energy returns, I feel I am (just) old enough to realize how extraordinary life is and that I'll never have to wear those frocks again.

Aitken Lawrie
I Would Like To Live Another
Twenty Years

AT THE moment I am fortunately fit and well. There are so many things I want to do that I would like to live for another twenty years, but this is not likely to happen. I do not want to end up in a nursing home in this sad, cold country where I can see all standards drifting rapidly downhill – art, music, literature, morals, honesty, dress, behaviour, education, discipline, travel, politics, etc. etc.

There have been many democracies in the history of the world, and they have all ended like this. Once power gets into the hands of an illiterate mob there is no hope for a country. I can do nothing to stop the rot, so the best thing I can do is desert the sinking ship and start a new life and a new career in Brazil in a warmer climate with plenty of willing staff to look after me.

It will be terribly sad to say goodbye to my family, but I hope they will be able to come out and stay with me from time to time and that they will be spared the responsibility of dealing with me in my old age. Luckily, all my children and grandchildren are coping well with their lives.

Initially, my new career will be to start a School of Bridge in Fortaleza. I began to give lessons when I was there earlier this year and found people keen to learn. But I must brush up my Portuguese.

Last year I had six holidays and was able to visit lots of beautiful places and paint them. Now there is nowhere else I want to see. I flew up to Scotland this summer to paint castles, which I really enjoyed. Then I hired a gallery in Guildford to exhibit nearly two hundred paintings. This went well.

I have had a wonderful life so far, mainly because I had a marvellous wife for nearly fifty years, four delightful children and eight promising grandchildren.

FIFTY PLUS FOUR

COLE PORTER wrote that the 'fountain of youth was a mixture of gin and vermouth', but who cares, why cling on to illusions, what's the point of being young at heart, who's fooled by looking good for your age? Let the fountain of youth splash away in some untended corner of the garden. I've always liked older people. I was at twenty more like sixty, and have never seen the point of taking formal exercise or combing the thinning hair over the bald patch. The older people are, the more fun they are. They've seen life, they know things the rest of us don't: they are unfazed and unfussed by the world's vagaries. Growing older increases pleasure. Novelty is not the only fillip to the palate; and understanding goes a long way to heighten the sensation. I think this is as true of eating, travelling or making love as it is of reading and listening to music.

The young have firm flesh and sometimes firm skin, enthusiasm and sometimes innocence, but they can be shallow, callow and self-centred. Age doesn't necessarily bring on ennui and cynicism. The other day a friend brought three people to lunch whose combined ages only narrowly added up to less than three hundred years, and we all had a picnic in an old orangery. All three of these nonagenarians (actually two nonagenarians and a centenarian) were sprightly of both mind and body, and a jollier lunch party you could scarcely imagine. The talk was of current affairs both governmental and social, there was a little reminiscing; there were good manners, a real enjoyment in the food and drink, ideas were batted about and good-natured gossip abounded. No one pretended to being one day younger than their real age, and no-one could have cared less. In my view, a table composed of pretty people in their twenties would have looked lovely, but oh! how bored I'd have been after a quarter of an hour.

There's some epithet that plays on the words of time and love, suggesting that the older we get the less loving we do, but I think love affairs are more fun once those painful early pangs are passed. Age knows more about the subjects in all its branches, it knows how to handle things, how to play along, and although you can be just as besotted, you don't get hurt so badly. The idea of throwing everything up to rush off and live with someone forever continues to have its appeal, but you know how to control the urge to do so, how to keep yourself in check, and the dividends this knowledge brings result in a gentler fall.

I fall rather into the cynical box, I must admit, and have a firm belief in the intransigence of more or less everything, but where that cannot be denied is in the simple fact that youth lasts a very short time. Embrace growing older, recognize all the advantages that age brings, clean your teeth and trim your nails but eschew the anti-wrinkle cream and the hair dye. Befriend as many people older than yourself as you can, and you'll really reap the benefits of their experience of life and have a jolly good time with them too. Let's scrap the cult of youth!

PADDY LEIGH FERMOR
NO OTHER EXPLANATION

LETTER TO THE EDITOR:

Dearest Susanna,

The moment I got to London, I set out with my piece in my hand to get it photocopied in Westbourne Grove. But when I got to the shop the sheet of paper had vanished! Into thin air! The only explanation I can find is that an inquisitive cherub had got wind of it, slid it from my grasp and winged away with it through the clouds. No other explanation. I write in sackcloth and ashes. I was ninety the other day but feel no wiser.

Antony Little
Nature Is Eternal

IN TERMS of age appreciation, I am a hopeless failure, which disqualifies me from making any contribution to this book.

When I was a child I did not feel particularly young, only wary of my short trousers and now that I am old will only be aware of old age when I perambulate in a bath chair.

The summer of adolescence and early adulthood, sex, drugs and rock and roll, followed by getting rich quick, which took all of three days to acclimatize to and appeared to me par for the course.

The autumn years of being grown up only confirmed to me what has been misnamed as civilization is nothing more than the human biomass rape of the natural world.

In the winter of old age the realization of the infinite breadth and time of the evolving world, a life is an insignificant wink of an eye and of no importance.

No doubt, dear reader, you may pity me for having missed the seasons of life, but I count myself lucky to be a failure. Not for me the pangs of youth or the bewilderment of senility, I'm just a straight-liner.

The reason for this is even worse. I am an emotional cripple and even hate the human race, but curiously I do have many friends I really like and love, and I find it a bit odd that they like me too.

I do feel very close to nature and being with nature is my life, nature is eternal. Beautiful and un-aggressive, even in the tide of human biomass that storms its every refuge.

My loathing is also because of its emotional religious dependency, people more intelligent than me believe in completely different Gods each believing their God is the only God and will kill for him, her or it, and God knows why.

I hate religious funerals and memorials; they cloud my memory of people I loved. God is the object of the ritual and one's dear departed merely as an excuse for some ecclesiastical cant.

On the bright side, I have a loving wife of forty years, a nice house in London. We spend our summers at our lodge and rolling acres in deepest Wiltshire and winters at our villa and land on Cape Peninsular in Africa.

This is the only time I have thought of any age awareness in any quantifiable entity and I have found I have none. You may think something is missing. But I don't think I would have been a good poet, do you?

RODDY LLEWELLYN
YOUNG RODDY

WE ARE all supposed to be 'middle-aged' at the age of forty. As I write this piece I am fifty-seven and feel roughly the same as I did in my late teens – except when I look into the mirror. Because I wet shave I stare at new lines and extending crow's feet every day, as well as the other signs of ageing like the eyebrows that now consist of tougher, more brittle hairs that decide to grow very fast and in every possible direction.

Nasal and aural hair require constant attention, my joints are stiffer when I get out of bed every morning, and sometimes I feel dizzy when I cut my toenails. I can't read the A to Z of London anymore except with a magnifying glass and need glasses for driving and the cinema. A friend, slightly older, always carries a bag with him when he goes for a walk in case anything falls off en route.

I have to be very grateful for the fact that my hair, now 'pepper and salt', has not receded and there is little sign of a bald patch. I am aware, however, that there is quite a lot of flesh travelling south and that my skin wrinkles in a different sort of way. I have one 'age spot' on the back of my hand.

From now on I suppose I have to look forward to further, gradual disintegration, but it doesn't bother me, as there is nothing I can do about it. I do care how I look but I feel that it is better to grow old graciously and with dignity rather than resort to the scalpel. There's something really rather ridiculous about faces that have obviously had surgery with botox lips stuck in an expressionless grimace.

I was once given a bit of very good advice by my Aunt Betty who, as I write, is as bright as a button, aged ninety. She stressed the importance of keeping your mind healthy when most other people seem to seek eternal youth at the gym. So, I bury myself in general knowledge, as well as cryptic crosswords and read and write as much as I am able. However, I also go to the gym two or three times a week, mainly to keep my heartbeat healthy. The art of conquering boredom in the gym is to ignore everyone else there, so far as it is possible, and to use the time usefully by thinking, something I find difficult to do at home and in the office, where there are constant distractions. I also use a moisturizer on my face. It is called 'Gentleman's Pride' and contains Aloe Vera.

I refuse to let life get me down and try to find the amusing side to everything. This is not always possible, but I strive towards it. I am emerging from a mid-life crisis with my sense of humour intact. The mid-life crisis should not be underestimated. A fight against the inevitable, the reluctant transition from what remains of your youth to middle age, is not easy to handle. At the end of it you are supposed to be 'grown up', but I am determined not to allow myself to become too disillusioned or cynical, grumpy or intolerant. In my case, I am not allowed to indulge in any of them when my young daughters are at home.

I spend quite some time out in the garden. I feel sure it helps to keep me trimmer than I would otherwise be, if only because I have to make countless journeys to and from the potting shed to retrieve a forgotten tool. They say that 'you are what you eat'. I am blessed with a wonderful wife (since 1981) who cooks delicious and nutritious food. The likes of 'organic' vegetables, fruit and oily fish are encouraged; fried fare of any sort is seldom if ever seen on the table. I always have in the back of my mind Nanny's wise words about food in general 'A little bit of everything does you no harm.' Nanny is ninety-five as I write and as well as can be.

I have been very lucky to have been able to make my love of plants into a profession. There is always a new plant to discover and try out. Horticulture is an indefatigable subject with fresh surprises around every corner; there is nothing humdrum about it. It is easy to remain enthusiastic and motivated because it is a subject I love. Perhaps that is the main reason why I have stayed young at heart.

OLD AGE HIT ME IN MY LATE TEENS

OLD age hit me in my late teens since, like many only children, I had been a stranger to people of my own age and as a child was held up as a remarkable example of maturity. My first real memory of this was at the age of six: I used to be summoned to the drawing room by my mother to mix the Negronis before dinner to the doubtless forced applause of her friends. So I think that what I dread now, when I suppose I have mentally reached my actual age, is that I will tumble into an inappropriate youth.

Of course the telltale signs of senescence are present, and *indomita mors* is more often in one's thoughts, but perhaps this will not lessen the risk of tumbling into second childhood. Increasing years bring the advantages and disadvantages of experience. Perhaps one expects less and consequently has fewer disappointments. The few disadvantages that one has are always made trivial by the awareness of one's good fortune.

Oddly enough, a greater acceptance of the ups and downs of fortune does not seem to have increased my patience or lack of irritation over small incidents. I suffer fools less gladly than I ever did, though I do not expect them to act less foolishly!

A Georgian friend who lived in Rome and was a spiky, if learned, old maid had an amusing comment about old age. He said that one of the three great pleasures of life – the pleasures of the boudoir –

were, alas, no longer available. The pleasures of the table only produced indigestion, but malice was still a joy. For me the fact that I no longer enjoy the pleasures of the table as I did before is a particular blow since I have lost my sense of taste for red wine entirely, having accumulated many delicious bottles. As for the dwindling of the pleasures of the boudoir – that of course has its calming side. The joy of malice – which, alas, does exist – I am afraid has to be overcome since the older one gets the more unattractive it is.

JOHN LUCAS-TOOTH
I REMAIN STATIONARY

POLICEMEN appear to grow younger. It is said that Einstein, getting on a train at Paddington asked whether Oxford stopped at his train. This is exactly what I think about growing old: I remain stationary, and the world grows younger round me. I am not talking about the geriatric aches, pains and maladies mentioned by other contributors, as these are inevitable and unavoidable, but what goes on in the inner workings of the brain. I cannot believe that my soul and spirit are decaying. I am told that when one is grown up, 20,000 brain cells die every day never to be regenerated, but the only noticeable effect (barring illness or physical trauma) appears to be a reduced ability to perform what the computer calls 'multitasking'. I certainly cannot order from a menu, worry about whether I shall still get back in time from lunch and listen to a piece of gossip all at the same time, although I feel that I can do all these things adequately as long as I do them one after the other.

Ageing is all to do with the thermodynamic concept of entropy. Entropy is a precisely defined physical quantity and is a measure of disorder and increases with every spontaneous event. Cooling cups of coffee, mixing colours on a palette, shuffling cards, dissolving bath salt crystals and growing old are all examples of increasing entropy. The entropy concept rules out all hope of perpetual motion machines. The second law of thermodynamics, which is quoted by everybody but rarely understood, encapsulates the concept with the formula $S = \ H/T$: a much more elegant and sensuous formula than the brutal $E = m.c.^2$. You cannot escape the constant erosion of entropy, whereas the nuclear bomb and the furnace of the sun may pass you by – Venus as opposed to Mars.

My adorable, lithe and skinny, grey and beige whippet also rides on Einstein's train. Although her train travels at seven times the speed of mine, our scheduled arrival times at Death Terminal are similar, which means at this moment she should have completed barely a third of her trip. Does she enjoy life more than me? Does her lack of experience give her more optimism than me or is she more confused by immaturity? I am not talking of trivial experience. She well knows that she can catch a squirrel in open ground but realizes that a thrush sitting on the lawn is almost pointless to pursue just as I, hearing the train going over the bridge at Didcot while I am still buying my ticket, know that I will have missed it. This comparison is in the same category as the aches and pains section.

What I am talking about is the realization that in old age there is either not enough time left to achieve a goal or that one's inherent abilities, even with acquired wisdom and application, are not up to the task. When one was young and professed an undying ambition to be an engine driver it also appeared to be equally possible to be a cabinet minister, a high court judge or a billionaire. Now I know that these achievements are not only impossible at the late stage I have now reached in life but were also never possible. It is a more complicated concept than a reduction in ambition because the 'engine driver' aim implies a great deal of constructive application. What gives my whippet such serenity in youth is that she is not fighting to get her entry ticket into Crufts.

This is not a council of despair or a cause of depression. The world is such a magical place that, provided we maintain an undying curiosity about both the great unresolved mysteries of existence and the many new ideas to which one is exposed every day, the fact that the physicists 'Great Unified Theory of Everything' will certainly escape me is an exciting spur rather than a lost cause.

A friend said to me that when he was a young man he thought about sex every few minutes but now he is old this is no longer a preoccupation. He said that it gives him a wonderful amount of spare time. Perhaps the motto for us old age pensioners is that old saying: 'dogs bark but the caravan goes on'.

Candida Lycett Green
What's Wrong With Now?

'DO YOU remember when…?' These are words I dread. For a start I *don't* usually remember, and anyway, why linger for any length of time in that other country, the past.? What's wrong with now? My lifelong friends Christopher Logue and Michael White are my paragons because they *never* talk about the past. Nostalgia's mawkish hand hasn't touched them. They are without prejudice, shocked by nothing. They embrace new things and are always on the trail of discovery. I try to emulate them. That's hard.

There are moments of silence: not restful ones but big, hollow, empty ones. Melancholy hangs over you like a storm cloud, and the words of Peggy Lee's song 'Is That All There Is?' echo on and on. That's bad.

The worst bit is the friends dying. But you love those remaining harder and deeper as a result. You experience things with more intensity, as though you are refreshing reality. Sunsets are more beautiful than they ever were before, and you tend to cry in films. So while the body packs up, the depth of feeling and the capacity for compassion grows. That's good.

The mantle of self-preservation which was wrapped around you as a parent of young children falls away, and a sense of recklessness floods back. You begin to say 'Yes' instead of 'No'. You agree to ride a wild horse, ski down a precipice. That's dangerous.

You have to work at age like you have to work at marriage: feeding it with what it needs. The bursting hope of youth becomes a tangible and necessary tonic. Music is another. A good 'dance up' sets me up for days, and I still feel the same old thrill listening to Ray Charles singing 'Ruby' as I did when I first heard it at fourteen. (Actually the feeling is bigger and stronger.) Having to earn a living is another. I'm bloody lucky in that. A doctor told me that stress caused through being over-busy (not the traumatic sort of stress which brings you down) releases a hormone called dehydroepiandrosterone (DHEA), which is meant to give you better brain and body function, boost your immune system and improve your complexion. (Can this really be true?) Then there is always the Monday-night poker game in the pub. Picking up a poker hand is one of the greatest adrenalin rushes I know. That doesn't diminish.

So nothing changes much. The inadvertent moving to the wings, as youth takes its rightful place in the centre of the stage, is a gentle, languorous transition. You feel grateful to be playing a bit part rather than a leading role. There aren't so many lines to learn for a start, and the roaring energy isn't always on tap. Meanwhile *I* don't change. I am still eighteen inside my head, even if bits of my body ache, chunks of my memory hang back, and I have to search harder than ever in Top Shop to find the mutton clothes.

Talking of clothes, I sat next to Hardy Amies at a *Vogue* Christmas party a few years back, and he told me he was eighty-seven. My consternation was genuine.

'How do you look so fine and dandy? What's your secret?' I asked.

'Sex, darling, regular sex,' he replied.

Another Grand Old Man, Milton Shulman, told Alan Watkins that there were two things that he was far better at in his sixties than when he was younger.

'What are they?' asked Alan,

'Tennis and fucking,' came the answer.

But it's my dad, John Betjeman, ever part of me, who must have the last word with his poem 'The Last Laugh':

> I made hay while the sun shone,
> My work sold.
> Now, if the harvest is over
> And the world cold,
> Give me the bonus of laughter
> As I lose hold.

RUPERT LYCETT GREEN
I Don't Believe In Old Age

I DON'T believe in old age, though I accept death, decay and illness. Olympic sprinter Linford Christie, still winning medals in his late thirties, said: 'Age is only a number.' It once turned out that Linford was running faster with a little help from his friends, but I think that, numerically at least, he was on the right track. And Edward Sturges, who ran his famous Pavilion Road gym commando-style for decades, sometimes leaving small boys hanging on the wall-bars for minutes at a time while distraught Knightsbridge nannies hovered nearby, could show you octogenarian ladies who, having taken up exercise once they got the great-grandchildren out of their hair, were skipping about like spring chickens in no time flat.

So age is just a mindset – wish yourself into a wheelchair and, accidents apart, you can easily wake up in one come Monday morning.

Two of my friends and contemporaries, both in their seventh decade and both in wheelchairs from riding accidents, take the opposite view. Their lives are shining examples of a timeless spirit of enterprise that makes a mockery of old age. Bill Shand Kydd, a paraplegic for eight years, recently launched himself earthwards on a stout parachute from an aeroplane flying at 10,000 feet. He did it for charity and merely noted to awestruck bystanders that should he die more money would definitely be raised. Chris Wolverton broke his

163

neck forty-three years ago. Since then, with his rickety wheelchair bundled into the boot of his car, Chris has travelled to France innumerable times to watch his horses race. Whether they win or not, Chris usually sets off after a good dinner to drive back to London via ferry or Channel Tunnel. It sounds tiring, and it is. I know that when I went with him he drove all the way there and most of the way home as I slumbered in the passenger seat. Chris is slowing down a bit, though. He recently retired from running his commercial property business to really concentrate on horses.

However, I have to admit that the passing of time does bring changes in its wake. When I was younger I worked in the West End in Dover Street, and from there up to Oxford Street on spring days there was more human beauty to be seen than, well, anywhere. But, whereas an admiring stare could get you a number of varying reactions if the recipient became aware of it then, now when they remake *The Invisible Man*, I shall hope for at least a stand-in role. For the comedy of growing old is not infirmity or death. It is that one is still so young. At the very end I would like to go out like Professor Juan Oro, who pioneered research into the origins of life. 'We are only stardust,' he smiled. 'I'm happy to return to the stars.'

PETER MATTINGLEY
AGE FIFTY-FOUR

DAD used to get up early, bicycle to Littleworth, milk half a dozen cows and be home in time to set off for work by seven-thirty. In the evenings and at weekends he was the town chimney sweep, part-time gravedigger and hair trimmer and cutter. He would carry a four-ten shotgun with him on his bike and poach Robert Heber Percy's pheasants. Dad also kept ferrets for catching rabbits, so we never went hungry. He was a character but a hard man. He liked his dog and would look after it well, but when it was no longer of use, he'd shoot it. He didn't seem to have any time for sentiment. Dad had been through a war; and four years in Burma would have aged Peter Pan.

Both my parents were severe. Once I went with my younger sister to catch newts. My sister fooled about, fell into the water and ran home covered in green slime. She told my mother that I'd pushed her, so I was given a caning on the spot. When my father came home he gave me another caning. Later I quietly sorted my sister out, and we didn't speak for weeks. That's childhood.

I always wanted to be a herdsman. I used to go milking every weekend and all through the summer holidays – that and helping Dad with grave digging – but my parents talked me out of it.

Thanks to Dad, I imagine, I had a need to apply myself.

One of my biggest thrills was being presented with a book for Sunday school attendance.

My mum died when I was thirteen. Her death was drawn out so, although it was very sad, we were well prepared. From then on, I became self-sufficient and cautious. I learned to take everything as it came and never to feel any envy for anyone else.

I left school at fifteen and started a five-year apprenticeship as a painter and decorator. It was then, while painting the outside of a house, perched on a ladder, that the lady of the house appeared naked from the bathroom. I had only seen pictures of naked ladies before. I was excited, scared and shaking from head to toe. Was this what life was going to be like? I've waited nearly forty years for a repeat. At the same time I attended Swindon College one day and two nights a week for five years in order to get my City and Guilds Certificate.

I fell in love with Jane – my lovely wife – one autumn but decided not to court her in earnest until after Christmas. I used to go out drinking then and hadn't enough money to buy her a Christmas present.

My start in life prepared me for the very happy life I lead today – now well into my second half-century.

The great advantage to getting older is that you know more: not only about your skill but also about communication with people. You feel more confident – a lot more.

It's important to see things from other people's point of view. If, for example, close friends decided to leave the neighbourhood, it's no use moaning that one's going to miss them. It's more worthwhile to think of them in their new life and to hope they're going to be happy.

I'm a painter and decorator. I love it. Absolutely love it. I couldn't have gone through life with a job I didn't enjoy. There is such huge variety. Sometimes I'm outside painting barns and farm buildings; sometimes I'm embellishing a lady's boudoir. I love going up a ladder, love a laugh and a chat, but I never let anybody get the better of me. It's a solitary job. I listen to the radio as I work. Discussions mainly. You learn a lot that way. Yesterday I heard that it was John Julius Norwich's birthday. Seventy-five. You'd never guess it.

I'm mad about sport. Any sport – mainly football. I'm a season ticket holder at Swindon. I play five-a-side football once a week at the Faringdon Leisure Centre and outdoor eleven-a-side football for a veteran team.

I eat well, keep fit and find age totally unimportant. My wonderful wife and children have all been blessed with the work ethic. The past, the present and the future are all part of the same story.

EARL MCGRATH
A WISE OLD NINETEEN-YEAR-OLD

I HAVE twenty-five godchildren, the oldest of whom is forty-six. I am seventy-three and have been married to my wife, Camilla, for forty-two years. She has always treated me as she would treat a twenty-five-year-old, as I was when I met her.

Also when I was twenty-five, my best friend was a musical person named Samuel Chotinoff, seventy years old. He treated me as if I was also seventy years old. His wife Pauline treated me as if I was eighty years old and a bad influence on her husband, my mentor.

So I always had mostly older friends until I was in my mid-thirties, when some of my godchildren became teenagers.

And then I had almost all of my older friends (some died) and an ever-growing group of younger friends and younger friends and younger friends and younger friends…a virtual 'pool' of helpers, employees, assistants, companions and teachers.

And they helped me to get older and stay younger, both at the same time. Now I feel like a wise old nineteen-year-old (somehow knowing that's how I started)…and it only hurts when I move.

That's it in a nutshell – where I belong.

DEBORAH MACMILLAN

GETTING OLD

I DIDN'T mind about getting old when I had to resort to glasses for reading. I thought that they made me look a bit more serious; but when I had to wear them to shave my legs, I thought that it was the beginning of the end. My mother thinks 'old' means having to sit down to remove your knickers. At eighty-five she is still standing to take them off and sometimes kicks them into the air, where they end up draped over the furniture.

When quite young, I often shot things, I am ashamed to admit – creatures: rabbits and kangaroos. Now I am truly soppy and can't kill anything except slugs and snails and fleas and ticks on the dogs. There are more of those than there should be as well – dogs that is, as I was unable to get rid of any of the pups from the last litter, and they run my life. I console myself at the over-catering because they are very good in bed and when people are appalled at the idea of umpteen Maltese even being allowed on the bed, I reply that if God hadn't meant dogs to be on the bed he wouldn't have given them a temperature of 101 degrees.

I have become a complete pushover, being repeatedly conned at the front door by the manure man and someone selling fish off the back of a truck. I have masses of steaming horseshit in the garden and piles of what I was assured were sea bass but taste suspiciously like Coley, in the freezer. As one grandmother went quite gaga and was once found cooking pieces of carpet, I suppose that I should be grateful that the manure isn't in the fridge and the fish on the flowerbeds.

One good thing about being older is that I no longer mind what people think. I didn't even blush when a security man at Copenhagen Airport found a forgotten lump of uneaten steak in my handbag. I had taken it home from a restaurant – for the dogs of course. It probably looked like Semtex. I looked helpless, and he listened pityingly to my explanation. Thank God it wasn't Washington.

For a long time I've avoided computers. This year my daughter tried to teach me how to use one. It was absolutely ghastly. Telling me that the computer I had was 'made by idiots for idiots', she forbad me to take notes, looked aghast when I could retain nothing, ignored my bleat that I was from the note-taking generation, spoke to me as if I were foreign and wondered why I spent the first weekend sending emails to myself.

I have at last mastered email and now can even delete the endless offers of Viagra and penis enlargement that bombard my machine.

Last year, I got my bus pass. It has been quite thrilling, buzzing around for almost nothing. I just hope that I can continue to remember where I am going, as I have almost forgotten where I have been.

VERY LATE YOUTH

As IT happened, the request to contribute to this volume arrived during my struggle to write a book on getting old. I am an optimist, the glass is always half full, rather than half empty, but I have never seen the point of trying to 'fight back' against the acceptance of the lined and balding head in the bathroom mirror. I would never jog or wade into the freezing sea at Brighton on New Year's Day. I prefer to exploit old age in our admittedly fairly early acquaintanceship but, at seventy-eight, I feel unable to claim any right to 'Late Youth'.

It's more 'pros' and 'cons' approaching eighty, and what I'll do here is list them both alternatively, but believing the former outnumber the latter.

Pro: Sustained friendships of both sexes. Those who were there.

Mick Mulligan, for one: my first bandleader (for twelve years). Conspirator in defying our roots and behaving badly. Happily married now, in a fine house and walled garden, part of the racing world, but when we meet the old are young, our intentions priapic and alcoholic, our mates and enemies resurrected.

Andy Garnett, no longer spry, a flat-mate who, in the fifties, was part of the less well-behaved Chelsea set and set off in his bubble car to invade the seedier aspects of the East End. Always a formidable raconteur, he remains one, despite having made several fortunes and recently invented and supported an imaginative good cause for no-hope kids in the Bristol slums. I love him.

Only a sample of those with whom I am able to wander down a memory lane.

And women? Mostly ex-girlfriends, now elderly ladies but unwilling to deny long-past nights. They are from all walks of life – posh to working-class. In our heads we are back in various beds, up against walls, in country houses, open fields illuminated unexpectedly by blast furnaces or on studio couches after Sunday lunch.

One-night stands too, and moments of fetishism where I was always willing to oblige.

Con: The sex act is now impractical, but...

Pro: The eye and the imagination are still in working order. No young woman could tell, I hope, that this elderly, tortoise-like figure was imagining scenes of frantic and instant lust.

Pro: My almost life-long atheism. This positive rejection of what Peter Nichols, the playwright, has called 'the paranoid rugger-player in the sky', the conviction that heaven and hell, purgatory and judgement don't and never have existed, that not only physical but personal death is final, are a great comfort. I don't fear death, that arbitrary old fool with a scythe, although, like Woody Allen, 'I don't want to be there when it happens.'

I've recently signed a 'living will', which doesn't allow medics to kill you but forbids them to keep you alive when what they call 'the quality of life' is gone. To avoid forgetting everybody and everything, not having to metamorphose into an angry, dribbling old doubly-incontinent vegetable is a double *pro*. The existence of children and grandchildren to carry one's genes into the future is, while I don't envy the poor things, a *pro* of some kind.

Con: Sly assaults of old age: an irregular heartbeat, chronic bronchitis, the retention of water, emphysema and a cornucopia of multi-coloured drugs to keep them at bay. The most irritating thing is the nightly diuretic pill, which means having to pee about eight times per night. A cancer that proved a false alarm (hurray), but it turned out to be emphysema (boo), and after fifty years committed to nicotine I've had to give it up. Some of the pills are so strong I'm obliged to have monthly blood tests. I call St Mary's Hospital 'Dracula's Castle'.

Pro: Surprisingly, though, my blood pressure and, even more extraordinary, my *liver* are in good nick – I think I'll pour myself an Irish whiskey right now. Delicious!

Another *pro* is that, after forty years of marriage, and undoubtedly irritated by my escalating deafness and colander-like forgetfulness, my wife shows no sign of treating me like King Lear and driving me out into Holland Park. On the contrary, she arranges 'treats' and does a lot of work dealing with business and keeping me up to the mark.

I've become obsessed with sleep. The cool pillow and the warm duvet have taken the place of active sex, although my eyes and brain are still in lecherous working order.

Jazz and Surrealism, tin gods of my adolescence, remain as necessary as the days grow few. Fishing too is as obsessive as ever. I went out recently, after several months off due to a strained back muscle, and landed two big trout. Bliss!

I have to agree with the great Billie Holiday, who sang 'I ain't got no future but Lord, Lord what a past.' I think of myself, however, as a cross-dressed Edith Piaf.

CHRISTOPHER MILES
FORTY YEARS ON...OR IS IT SIXTY?

LOOKING at the receding planet of Mars in a recent starlit Wiltshire sky, I thought of the old cliché about the insignificance of man and a remark made to me over a decade ago by the film director Lindsay Anderson as we handed out student film prizes at the French Institute. 'Who really cares?' he said.

My first thought was 'Well, *they* do', meaning the students, and then I thought of all the young people who had worked on these efforts. Lindsay was nearing seventy then, and his face wore the look of a tired, empty man that evening; and although we have both had our successes and failures, and the slings and arrows of outrageous cinematic fortune have hit us hard sometimes, I still felt that I cared.

I care for my family and relations, my close friends and what I am trying to do with the rest of my life. They say you are born with a positive attitude (or not), it's all in the genes and that there's nothing you can do to change it. This may be so, but since having my first film on the BBC as a twelve-year-old, I have always known what I enjoyed most. If you can turn that enjoyment into a career, then you are lucky.

Film directors don't retire, they just drop off their canvas chairs. Age has no effect. A recent film that I shot in the beautiful setting of Stanway House, *The Clandestine Marriage*, was saved from financial ruin by Joan Collins, a sprightly seventy-year-old.

Noel Coward said he preferred 'a good book and an apple' to sex. Age, for most of us, whittles away that urge, but it's delightful to put the book down occasionally.

A garden can also keep you happy and busy, as it does for my wife Suzy and daughter Sophie, both talented painters. Without their support during thirty-seven years of married life, I would have had difficulty in surviving the non-existent British film industry.

Occasionally I try sketching to keep my hand in, as I sometimes have to draw elements of the script I am working on into a 'storyboard' to try to explain to other departments what's in my head before filming.

Recently I have busied myself diverting a stream at the bottom of our field to make a small island. And even in the piercing ultraviolet heat of this dry summer, the water plants have survived. It's been a good year for fruit as well. The apples are looking rosy…so I think I shall eat one and take a good book (probably a script), wear a sun hat and enjoy the coming weekend…

JOHN JULIUS NORWICH
DISTINCTLY PLEASURABLE

I'M seventy-five, and I mind it far, far less than I thought I would. I think the first secret is to accept the inevitable; just don't think about it at all, neither complaining of the increasing aches and pains and various incapacities that are bound to occur nor fighting too hard against them. The one indulgence that I do allow myself is regular checkups: two or three a year. I don't see this as hypochondria, merely as giving the machine regular servicing as one does one's car and, if something is going wrong, nipping it in the bud.

I hate walking – though I probably do it for half an hour a day, largely to and from tube stations – but I do struggle for twenty minutes on an exercise machine every morning just to keep the blood circulating. I try, with varying degrees of success, to keep the weight down, but I'm naturally greedy, and I make no effort to reduce my intake of wine, which is far greater than most people would say was good for me but seems – thank God – to suit me remarkably well. The really important thing, I think, is to exercise the brain. I'm so relieved that for the past forty years I have been self-employed, so that there can be no question of retirement on pension and subsequent condemnation to the golf links. (Frankly I'd prefer the galleys.) I shall continue to write – indeed I shall have to – for as long as I can hold a pen or see the laptop screen.

I find certain aspects of old age distinctly pleasurable. It's lovely reducing one's ambitions, facing up to having missed doing things one always thought one wanted to do and not really minding a bit. I now know that I shall never make a parachute jump, never trek in the Himalayas (too hard on knees and ankles), never again water ski – or snow ski for that matter. I thought I should never get on a horse again, but to my great surprise found myself on one this summer in Montana – fortunately with one of those lovely western saddles with a pommel to hold on to. I still want to visit all the places in the world that I haven't been to – much of South America, most of Central Asia and the South Seas – and have every intention of travelling till I drop; but I am beginning to face up to the fact that I don't really want to rough it much anymore; hot baths and good dinners after a long day are, I fear, a great deal more important than they used to be. After all, it's fun to cosset oneself. For my sixtieth birthday I replaced all my lace-up shoes with moccasins and slip-ons. Except for the occasional pair of reluctantly donned walking boots, it's a joy to reflect that I shall never again have to tie a pair of shoelaces.

And there's another, even happier, reflection; that one has *made it*. I can think of all too many of my contemporaries cut off in their prime for one reason or another; my own father died at only sixty-three. I, on the other hand, have notched up my three-score and ten and, I like to think, am still in pretty good shape: deaf as a post, but now at last with a really good pair of hearing aids, a few teeth gone but still able to chew, unable to remember names but with the majority of my marbles still more or less intact. I have a perfectly lovely wife and want it to go on as long as possible while I remain compos and continent and not a burden to Mollie or my children. The moment this happy state of affairs ceases to prevail, they all have strict orders to pull the plug on me at once; but even then I shall have no reason to complain. I consider myself to have already won the lottery of life. Nobody can take away those seventy-five marvellous years – and they should be enough for anyone.

JOHN OGDEN

THE WALKING STICK

MY THIRTIETH birthday was the worst, the hardest to face. Thirty already, I said to myself. Half my life gone, I expect, and what have I done? Oh God, how old I am. Youth gone. Infirmity imminent.

Forty was easier. I seemed calmer about the watershed. I had a few grey hairs. People occasionally took me seriously. Youth had gone, but maturity was beginning to have its rewards. I came to terms with my age and enjoyed myself.

Fifty was an achievement. Half a century of experience, I thought, that's worth a bit. I bought a book called *Life after Fifty* written by some American academics who assured me life would only get better. I believed them. The day came, marked by some cards, a small party and a few presents. Gifts, wrapped in fine paper and ribbon, are always welcome at any age. I sorted them into sizes and found the largest. It was long and thin. The label showed it was from my mother-in-law, a sparky beauty I would have liked to have been married to, if I hadn't married her daughter. She was sitting looking at me as I picked it up and started to unwrap it. It was a walking stick. It was, I must admit, an elegant walking stick that cannot have come cheap.

'A walking stick?' I said.

'A walking stick,' my mother-in-law echoed.

'Why a walking stick?'

'You're fifty now. You'll need a walking stick.'

'I don't need a walking stick.'

'You'll find it very useful.'

'I hope not.'

'Every man at your age should have a walking stick.'

'That depresses me.'

I put that stick in the umbrella stand in the cloakroom. Every day I saw it and said: 'Oh no you don't.' Years have passed. Sixty has come and gone. Seventy, too. My darling mother-in-law has died, aged ninety-one. Maybe I'll make ninety or even a hundred. I'm never going to use that walking stick. I still look at it daily and say: 'You're not getting me.'

MILO PARMOOR

IT'S A WONDERFUL START TO THE DAY

'JUST another five for me.' American techniques of motivation, interpreted by Chris of Leeds, my personal trainer, make the gym extremely agreeable. 'Terrific', 'Well done', 'That's it' and similar interjections of approval and support get me to exhaust my arms and legs on the grey and black machines, each provided with gauges of effort like kilometre per hour, distance moved, average speed, heartbeat, calories expended. It's a wonderful start to the day. I go at 7.15 a.m. and get back to my flat at about 9.00 after a few lengths of the pool and a wallow in the Jacuzzi. If he's not busy, Chris sometimes waves goodbye. If I miss the gym for a week or two, I go back to threes and fours on the resistance gauges instead of the sixes or sevens I'd been on. Those keen on historical justification might remember the Romans putting up baths everywhere they went.

'Twos and threes' are what an uncle, bursar of an Oxford college, used to call small pieces of firewood. He provided two bits of advice to see me through life neither of which I've so far had occasion to follow, and it's getting late. The first was 'never cut beyond possibility' – in answer to my question, he said that here 'possibility' meant estimated annual volumetric growth of timber in woodland. The second was 'buy Lincolnshire pea-farms to yield six and sell them to yield four'. In later years he travelled around with a special device inserted into the boot of his car for carrying claret over country roads.

I've more or less forgotten how to write legibly other than on a computer, but so far have worn neither a water bottle nor trainers (except in the gym). It's been a great time for life with aeroplanes, televisions, computers, mobile 'phones, emails, the vast improvement of motor cars and, with better food, of people's height and looks. Remember how short so many people were? And their complexions? My first car in the late 1940s (a Morris or was it an Austin?) was miserable in winter, as cold air came up through a floor punctured by the gear lever.

The thing I haven't much liked is the period notion that you can and should express a self, independent of time, place and instruction, excepting this one. Probably it's because I don't like it that I'm less modern about art. It should, I feel, be difficult to make: need training. It's not meant to be simply a premeditated con. Anselm Kiefer's leaden library – whether joke, allegory, symbol or something else – is beautifully detailed, must have been staggeringly expensive to make and elicits in me a shivering thrill of awed interest and excited admiration, but a lot isn't like that. It's often prosaic, *jejeune* and silly. The newspapers hopefully suggest that education policy may react against the idea that free slaves sprout unaided. Out of sync with displays of shabby imperial clothes, I relish the Gherkin, liked the Dome and still do the Jubilee line, love Bilbao and wish they'd do away with planning restrictions of any aesthetic sort.

Only in the last decade or so has London woken up. It took most of my life for the heart of the imperial corpse to show signs of life. Declining, even with Chris's help, into immobility, I hope to see the place forget that – crippled by nostalgia – it ever wanted to be a theme park and so get livelier, richer, more splendid and international. Roll on tomorrow; there's further fun, comfort, delight and better food and bodies round the corner – possibly, that is, of course. You have to be a little realistic.

DAVID PLANTE

A BEAMING AWARENESS ABOUT THE YOUNG

A FRIEND of my age, mid-sixties, tells me that whenever he sees a group of young people on a beach, their bodies bright, splashing about in the surf, he longs to go to them and say: 'You're young! You must know. You're young! You're young!' He feels that when he was young, if he had known he was, he would have enjoyed his youth, truly enjoyed it, as he regrets he didn't: as if knowing creates a beaming awareness about the young that must make being young wonderfully fulfilling in itself.

Though it is most often the ageing and the aged who believe this about the young, I remember moments when I did know I was young, and knowing did make me imagine I was blessed in my youth.

On a particular afternoon when I was, oh, around thirty – which, from over sixty is young – I was taken by Susanna Johnston and two of her daughters, Rosie and Silvy, on a picnic in an olive grove outside of Vinci, the little mountain town in Tuscany where Leonardo was born. The sunlight flashed through the branches of the olive trees as we lolled on an old oriental rug in the midst of cheeses and bread and fruit and, of course, a fiasco of glasses and spilled wine that seeped into the rug and elaborated the pattern, while I listened to Rosie playing her guitar and Silvy singing to me – singing to me because, I felt, I was one of them. Though I was, I admit, entirely self-centred in what I still considered my young years, I was not unaware that

Susanna was as young as I was, but my egotism was greater – she joined the girls in singing and enchanting me so I felt beamed with the awareness of everything being ahead of me in my life, everything being joyful simply because everything was possible (which, I suppose, is an idealization of youthful sensibility and an indication that, idealizing youth as I did, I was in fact far from young). The two beautiful girls went on enchanting by playing with a long, long, gold embroidered scarf wrapped about the shoulders of one, then both wrapped it about themselves in a tight cuddle. I was deluding myself, no doubt, but the delusion was powerful… I knew I was with them in all the wonder of their youth.

They brought me even closer to the centre of the wonder when, back in the Johnston house on a hillside outside Lucca, various other young people arrived, and I found myself playing sardines, crowded into a tiny dressing room with them (Susanna, roaming about the house, was searching for us), all of us trying to be still and silent, but not enough so, for Susanna found us quickly. The gang of young people (Susanna and I in their midst) gathered for dinner under the pergola, and there was talk of what to do later that summer night that resolved itself into a plan to go to a discotheque. Rosie and Silvy both pressed me ('Oh! Come on!') to go. Well, if their mother would come. But Susanna, smiling a slight smile, perhaps knowing something about the club that I didn't and amused by my innocence, which she would rather not witness the end of, said no, she'd stay behind. She might have thought that I was more innocent than I in fact was, however innocent in my youthfulness I did appear, for I became rather excited when Rosie and Silvy told me I wouldn't be allowed into the club unless I was heavily made up and wore something more seductive. I gave myself up to them, but because I worried that a shock of self-consciousness on saying that I really wasn't going would destroy me, I refused a looking glass. The sight of a tube of very dark purple lipstick approaching my lips did alarm me a little. I was given a very loose shirt printed all over with dancing girls

– that it had belonged to a former guest who died from an AIDS-related illness made me think all too vividly of little risks, not altogether innocent, I had taken in my real youth and of my early twenties, when living alone in Boston and going out every weekend to night clubs. The other young people went on ahead. I was left with Rosie and Silvy, who also were exotically made up and dressed. 'Do come,' I pleaded with Susanna, but all she did was smile, now somewhat compassionately. I went off in the car – I think, in the back seat – with the girls to the discotheque, called Frau Marlene, a large apparently prefabricated hanger of a club in a rubbish-filled field near Viareggio. I entered between the girls into a world of young people of, they'd told me, various sexes, including svelte drag queens with long glittering fingernails; and, among them all but within the parenthesis of my two partners, I did think: 'I'm young!' I danced with both girls in very close bodily proximity, one on each arm, and was annoyed whenever a presumptuous young man, presumably of a fixed sexuality that focussed exclusively on girls, pulled now Rosie and then Silvy from me on the crowded dance floor. This was competition, because I was, I felt, their age; and with Rosie and Silvy my sexuality was then as fixed and focussed as theirs. But the faithful girls always came back to me quickly, and I would stare at my competitors, who had managed to get into the club without makeup or fancy dress but on sheer good looks, with the confidence of being, if not better looking, then more attractive for being attractive to Rosie and Silvy than they were.

Then this happened, and old age began – Rosie was pulled away from me by a very good-looking youth – pulled away as if to show me his greater determination – and drew her off into a corner. Dancing with Silvy. I kept my eye on them, feeling, I must say, more than possessive, but protective of dear Rosie. I was relieved when she soon left him to return to me, now laughing and pointing back to the youth, who stood solid with his arms crossed and his face beautifully expressive of his superiority, and said to me, translating from the

Italian: 'He just asked me what the fuck are you doing here with your father?'

In my old age, I have given youth over entirely to the young, given it over with a sense of the triumph of the young in their youth; and the older I get the more I want to tell them – as my friend so wants when he sees the young exposed in all their beauty on a sun-bright beach, to tell them just how beautiful they are – that they are blessed simply for being young, and that they must – oh must! – fulfil all the wonders of that blessing.

Rex Pyke

Thousands Of Tomorrows
Have Sadly Passed

IN THE four years that we have known each other, Robin has managed to learn both English and Swedish while I have only managed '*tack*' in Swedish. I am sixty years older than his four. Soon there is going to be an endless series of crossovers, where in different spheres he will be capable of more and more, and I less. As he ascends, I will decline. Currently I am pretty good with Lego and his Brio wooden railway, but he is catching up fast. Yesterday, his imaginative creation of a Lego roll-on/roll-off ferry was truly brilliant. The real ideas are now coming from him.

Susanna's invitation to make this contribution has prompted me into suddenly thinking about something that up until now I haven't bothered with. I breeze through life confident of endless tomorrows. I have twenty-year-old newspapers that I can't throw away because I haven't read them yet. I have videos of the last part of late films that I can't manage to stay awake and watch. I really do believe I am going to actually read those papers and eventually view the films, the beginnings of which I have long since forgotten.

I suspect that if I ever find myself dying I will be totally surprised.

At ten years old I was, for a brief period, the youngest boy at my boarding school, and fifty-five years later that still remains with me.

David Puttnam once commented to Peter Hall: 'the trouble with Rex is that he thinks he is still a Boy Scout.' David was right. I still only do what I want to do, and it's always fun. In financial terms my life has been a series of lost opportunities: me going for the moment rather than the future.

I am always initiating projects but rarely completing them, always confident I will do it tomorrow but in the meantime going off at a tangent with something far more exciting – for that moment at least.

At a time when my contemporises are panting their way around the golf courses and moving into bungalows with a picture window and conservatory, I have bought a derelict four-storey tower. All I have done with it so far is to plant over a thousand trees, many of which are now hosting birds' nests. Hooray.

Instead of retiring, not only am I now making more films than ever, often several at the same time, but I have also started a parallel career as a professor at the University of Glasgow.

If there is a secret, it is to never worry about appearances. I have never owned a car that is valuable enough to have to insure comprehensively. I always wear the same sort of clothes. They have to be dark enough not to show the dirt and can be collectively chucked into any washing machine. I never worry about what to wear.

However, I did recently buy a suit. It came from an Oxfam shop in Oxford with funerals in mind. So there is a concession. Must get some black shoes. I am dismayed by the growing frequency. All women: Jill, Gloria, Sara and last week dear Lizzy.

I now have five grandchildren: all girls. One of my daughters observed that I was better at being a grandfather than a father. Probably because, with my children, I was always promising that I would give them my time tomorrow. Thousands of tomorrows have sadly passed.

I can't bear strangers doing things for me: hotel porters carrying a bag I could carry, or doctors and dentists fiddling with me. So I have always cut my own hair, unless I am living with someone who will do it for me.

Every now and then I am unexpectedly shocked by not being able to do something I had taken for granted, like push a car that is stuck in the snow or walk up a steep hill and walk and talk at the same time.

PAUL RABEN
I'M GLAD I'M NOT YOUNG ANYMORE

FREE of booze and fags – both formerly done to excess – I am healthier at fifty-five than I was at thirty-five. But I spend longer in the bathroom than I used to and with less effect. After fifty, nobody can dazzle, but one should try not to disgust. Head hair that was effortlessly springy in one's twenties now needs daily help to avoid looking like road-kill. Visible surplus hair elsewhere must be purged. My pet aversion – which I keep before my eyes as a 'never' (comparable to the warning pictures of fatties that people stick on the fridge door) is an old nose with growths hanging down like the beard of an oyster. Ear hair, less accessible, should not run to briar. One egregious offender in this regard sports horrid 'set-aside' whiskers on the cheekbones – resembling Denis Healey eyebrows stuck on by Magritte – but then he is a man who likes to slurp your wine around his gums and pronounce upon the vineyard. Face, nose, ears, eyes: all must be vigilantly checked for loose matter, vaguely endearing on the noon-risen teenager but repulsive on the adult. In my new flat a power shower has been made a priority, riot-police jets of hot water will be my early-morning ally.

Despite this effort, like most people of my age, I have ceased to exist to the young. It was not a process; it seemed to happen with sudden savagery – like the collapse into darkness of the African night. I began to notice with clammy horror that the well-meant pleasantry to young shop assistants was provoking a distant watchfulness as if making ready to repel looming lechery. I felt I had become at a stroke one of those sad old men who look as if they might make a nuisance of themselves in public parks. With heavy heart, I amended my shop patter, never straying now beyond businesslike courtesy. Amongst the young, I try to remember at all times that I will never again be of their number; attempts to ingratiate by behaving otherwise are grotesque. The penalty for forgetting this is invariably mortification. A forty-seven-year-old acquaintance of mine developed a crush on a girl of twenty-three. He suggested lunch, which went off all right, but when he proposed a dinner, she backed off sharply. Foolishly, he tried negotiation and, getting nowhere, lost all caution. 'If you went to bed with someone my age, you'd have the best sex you've ever had.' Into the proffered neck of the wounded bull she sank the matador's sword. 'Thanks, but I'd rather have bad sex with someone of my own age.' And so at her age would most people.

Compensations have arrived in swarms, but they are all developments of the mind not the body. I now know when meeting strangers that the seeds of friendship are either there or not, and if not then regret is pointless. I no longer perform acrobatics of personality to adapt myself to a fancied vision of what some attractive newcomer might prefer. I no longer feel obliged to laugh at what I don't find funny or what I don't understand. I have given up assuming a causeless grin when in casual talk or when being photographed. An unsmiling face is not necessarily a sombre face. A genuinely smiling face can be delightful, but a face in repose is usually more interesting. The sensible Victorians never counterfeited jollity before the lens. Imagine Lord Tennyson by Julia Margaret Cameron or Balzac by Nadar with their features creased into the rectal bonhomie of a cruise-ship grin (such as those customarily slapped on the mugs of Des O'Connor or Tony Blair), and one sees with a shudder the gimcrack nature of our pseudo-matey age.

Physical ailments must be quickly skipped over. I know of an otherwise easygoing host whose strict household rule is three permitted minutes on personal illness, whether it be terminal cancer or chilblains. Indifferent to sport, I nevertheless smile at the old French clubman who said he looked forward to dying at ninety-seven from a fall off a polo pony.

I see myself making all the same mistakes that my parents made, and I feel the acid of regret for my old harsh judgement of them: what I did not know at twenty-five – that others have the right to be wrong and that nobody ever wins an emotional argument, of which the sole payoff is acrimony. H. L. Mencken said his favourite escape method from heated arguments – particularly with fools – was to murmur affably: 'Well, you may be right.' I remain a fumbling student of the art of disagreeing gracefully. Above all, I am still learning that most things are none of my business.

His Phantasy Old Age

Absurd to contend that there is any merit in being old and getting older – save, the only alternative of course. But in my own case I claim each decade has been better than its predecessor; though in making that claim I see that I am vulnerable to the suggestion that I had a dull youth. More a case of feeling immensely freed from the cares and anxieties of youth. Too little care in old age: bumping carelessly not only into doorposts but into the sensitivities of one's old friends.

St John Clarke (A. Powell *passim*) asserted that 'growing old consists abundantly in growing young': a view attributed to him by his creator to emphasize his absurdity. So if Powell fans (and others) are to avoid this fate – absurdity – what to do?

A tendency to wear very short shorts, very tight shirts, very unsuitable clothes generally should be checked. Youthful coiffure is difficult for the balding and greying.

What's the chance of becoming a clean old man? Only good if the spouse is there to supervise it perhaps. One part of old age might be sauntering (I deleted 'tottering') down South Audley Street in a perfectly cut, perfectly clean but infinitely threadbare grey worsted suit, a clean shirt, a clean tie and polished shoes for a lunch of sweetbreads and a little claret.

Then a more rural fantasy of the infinitely arthritic and buckled old man hobbling out of his terminally decrepit and derelict mansion to welcome the last of the friends prepared to put up with a visit spent before flickering fires and between damp sheets, but with unexpectedly good claret which has to be drunk before the successor can claim it.

Broadly then, Walter Mittyesquely: phantasies will support me through the final stages, but the fires caused to glow will not be the ashes of youth.

STEVEN RUNCIMAN

By David Plante

Sir Steven Runciman, the great historian of Byzantium and the Crusades, was always keen to fulfil projects that sustained him into very old age – such as his project to visit each every one of the United States. He had almost fulfilled the project, including a visit to Alaska, where he became friendly with Russian Orthodox nuns, but was missing Oklahoma. For a brief period in the 1980s, I was teaching at the University of Tulsa and invited Steven to stay with me.

I waited for him outside Arrivals at the airport – he was coming in from Texas, where he had been entertained, including the gala first night at the opera, in a way I wouldn't be able to do, but Steven – as much as gala events excited him (he confessed he was shy, but he was unabashed describing such events) – never made me feel anything but special for whatever entertainment I could offer him. I looked for him among the disembarking passengers; he did not appear. I asked if all the passengers had disembarked, and was told 'yes'; and, thinking he had not been able to come, I was about to leave when I saw him standing by a small suitcase on wheels, wearing a summer suit that appeared too small for him, the trousers revealing his red and black ribbed socks. 'But I didn't see you among the passengers,' I said, to which he answered in the mock-haughty way he had: 'I appeared miraculously.' (He liked announcing that he had great powers.)

Over the three days that he spent with me, I showed him, by car, the sights of Tulsa, including the museum with Native American and pioneer artefacts. 'This isn't history,' he said, 'it's memory.' But he was now able to say that he had been to Oklahoma: to shift it from the States not visited to the almost all-inclusive list of those that he had. This was very satisfying. He insisted on buying many postcards.

I also gave him a drinks party. I invited a young drag queen I'd got to know. Never having met a drag queen before, or so he said so as not to disappoint me and my efforts to supply him with as many firsts as possible, Steven was curious. Called Danny as a young man, the drag queen called herself Doreen. She wore a backless dress that revealed her pimply back, and pointing at herself with a long red fingernail that was glued on askew, she informed us that she was the richest woman in Tulsa. Steven did the gentlemanly thing – kissed her extended hand. No doubt it was my presumption to think that, if I couldn't do more, my introducing Steven to the drag queen would supply him with material enough for an anecdote, of which he had many and which he recounted to great effect at dinner parties in London, although meeting a drag queen in Tulsa, Oklahoma hardly ranked with those about his playing piano duets with the last emperor of China or dancing with a woman who had danced with the Prince Consort. In fact, the drinks party I gave for Steven was rather dull, which he afterwards admitted, but he said to me: 'I'm always eager for a party. One never knows whom one will meet.' He was then in his late eighties.

In London I saw him when he came from his castle in Scotland for dinner parties, drinks parties, receptions; and these occasions he described vividly, with insights into them that I took to be those of someone utterly confident of his standing in society, such as: 'Invited to dinner at an embassy, I know, just by looking at the other guests, where – by protocol – my place at table will be.' He never turned down an invitation. Too frail to walk, he discovered, to his delight, the pleasures of a wheelchair, so he continued to come to London for all those social events, more and more in his honour, at which he might meet someone from a world he hadn't yet visited, perhaps from one of the very few States he hadn't been to: Arizona? North Dakota? He had been everywhere else in the world.

NIGEL RYAN
A CHANGE OF FOCUS

NOT so long ago I smiled at a pretty girl in the underground. She smiled back – and offered me her seat. At around the same time I began noticing that when I looked in the mirror expecting to see white teeth and brown hair an awful change was taking place; soon it would be the other way about.

This, then, was the downward slope. What I did not know was that it was all part of a process of liberation leading to the magic garden of second childhood.

The process dates back to the day when I watched the body of my 91-year-old father being put into a hole in the ground. Suddenly I became aware that one day this would happen to me. Rather late in life, you may think: but then my life has always seemed like a jigsaw with the pieces turning up in random order. The discovery set off a subtle but seismic shift, not so much in outside events or in my character: more a change of focus. But the point is that far from gloom, the shedding of illusion has brought quite unexpected dividends.

Also late in life (his this time, not mine) I met Isaiah Berlin. He was in his eighties but his genius for presenting profound truths with dazzling simplicity had not deserted him. I made a diary note:

A brief exchange on the stairs after dinner. IB not pleased, I thought, to be talking to me (wrong gender). I forget my question, doubtless

201

limp, about something overheard across the table. The answer came
back like machine-gun fire:

'Civilisation is peaceful coexistence between conflicting truths. Yes.'
He said it twice in the time it would take a normal person to say it once.
There was a short pause. Then:

'The lion has the right to his lunch. The lamb has the right to his
life. What is the solution to this dilemma? There isn't a solution: there
is only compromise. The lion must put up with some meatless days. The
lamb must be told, your life expectancy is not quite what you'd like it
to be. There is no perfect answer. There it is, there it is.'

And a final quick burst to see off the twin twentieth century heresies
of communism and facism (not to mention the up and coming
fundamentalism of the twenty-first):

'Political action can't change human nature. If anyone tells you that
he has the solution to the universe you must vote against him. For,
whether he knows it or not, he is a tyrant. Yes. A tyrant. Whether he
knows it or not. There it is.'

And down the stairs he went. I think he had spotted a lady he
wanted to sit with. I didn't mind. I had my nugget.

The change of focus was complete. Thanks to the great man I was
finally released from the tyranny of impossible expectations –
whether of myself or of the world. There were no perfect solutions.
There was no tidy jigsaw, so I could stop trying to fit the pieces
together. Far from solving the universe I was free to make the best of
its contradictions and surprises. I was a child again with my toys. And
in a child's eye the magic tends to be in the detail rather than the
grand design; so it is details that I have spent my own second
childhood collecting. I treasure them for the golden nuggets they are.

I was filming in Afghanistan during the Soviet invasion. The
civilian population was being bombed and starved. During an air raid
that nearly killed us all I came across an elderly couple trembling
uncontrollably beside a rock where they were sheltering. Too shocked

to veil her face the woman greeted me by offering, not once but twice, a scrap of bread clutched in her hand. I have never forgotten that instinctive gesture of hospitality still intact under the threat of annihilation; nor the woman's face, the only one I was to see throughout my visit. I hope I never shall: the memory of that fine fragment of human dignity is as precious to me – and every bit as grand – as my first sight of the Parthenon.

My latest nugget is Milly.

So far as I knew my immediate family ceased to breed several decades ago and I had assumed the blood line was destined to die out. Earlier this year I found out I was wrong. An elusive nephew arrived on my doorstep with a pretty Chinese wife (from Chungking) and a daughter called Milly. Milly turns out to be a bilingual four-year-old Einstein, and a life force. According to her mother she considers sleeping a waste of time, and has certainly no time to be shy. She threw aside a doll with a change of clothes that I bought her as a present, but pounced on a Babar the Elephant book and scanned it from cover to cover emitting a 'Wow!' (she goes to a Canadian school in Hong Kong). After tossing off a couple of Picassos for me she suggested a game of hide and seek (I won because she couldn't resist telling me where she was going to hide). Finally she consulted her mother in Mandarin about the hierarchical status of a great uncle and with a cry came out with the English version 'Crumbling Uncle!' I was absurdly flattered.

Since when I have been having second thoughts. Power may be fools' gold and Mr Blair's Third Way a blind alley: but perhaps after all a new and dynamic branch of Chinese Ryans will unlock the solution to the universe.

Me, I'm off to Cuba to search for more nuggets among its dilapidated splendours before the US fundamentalists get there.

JIMMY SKINNER

KEEPING A ZEST FOR LIFE

EVER since a bunch of monkeys developed self-consciousness, or, if you prefer it, ever since Adam tasted the Fruit from the Tree of Knowledge, human beings have had a problem. Why bother to get out of bed in the morning? What is the point of it all?

Nature provides an immediate answer. We want to stay alive, and we want our genes to continue forever. Our twin needs for survival and procreation compel us to climb out of bed for food – and back into it for sex. These two imperatives provide us with an absolutely basic, short-term motivation for action. But what about the long haul? Animals may find food and sex fill all their days quite satisfactorily, but humans fancy themselves as being more sophisticated than that. Each one of us feels somehow special – even if everyone else seems pretty ordinary.

The first symptom of self-consciousness is self-regard – narcissism develops at the moment of recognition in the mirror. Each individual becomes aware that he or she is, by definition, the centre of his or her own universe. Knowledge of our own individual uniqueness compels us to devise a structure to the universe into which we can fit neatly – in the centre. There are plenty of off-the-peg universal structures to choose from. They come mostly in the form of religions, designed to pander to our need to be reassured that we are special and not just 'here today and gone tomorrow'.

A well-chosen religion can provide a reassuringly stable structure. It identifies a hierarchy of authority with lists of 'dos' and 'don'ts' and rewards and punishments. A religious system can create order out of chaos for a lonely individual floating in a vast and incomprehensible universe. It can provide an object to life by promising a place in heaven to those who keep the rules. The details of heaven can be tailored to individual tastes (ranging from teams of virgins to caviar eaten to the sound of trumpets), but hell is usually more specific, with details of excruciating torture lovingly depicted by devout medieval artists.

All this provides the general background to the 'human condition', but what about the individual? What if you simply cannot swallow something so inherently improbable as religion? Religious faith, like any other kind of motivation, is something you either have or you don't. You cannot make yourself into a believer through willpower, any more than you can manufacture an interest in that which you find utterly boring. Something has to happen inside your mind to deflect the focus of your attention away from yourself and onto something else that is able to absorb your interest completely.

Motivation is a mystery. Some teachers have the magic gift, and their pupils flourish as a subject is brought to life in front of their eyes. What makes something fascinating to one person when everybody else is bored stiff by it? A train-spotter in an anorak is a puzzle for anyone who believes that trains are just devices for getting you from A to B. Most people have their own special passion in life, and the range is infinitely varied.

But we are looking for more than just hobbies to keep us actively engaged with life until the end. Ultimately, the most absorbing subject of all is life itself and the wonder and curiosity it inspires until the very end. Dr Johnson meant more than a compliment to London when he made his famous remark that 'a man who is tired of London is tired of life'. London is symbolic of human affairs and their infinite complexity and fascination. Humans interact with one another in ways that keep our minds and emotions constantly engaged.

But that is only one side of the wonderful and intriguing labyrinth of life. To many people, nature – meaning all living things on earth and their relation to each other and the universe – is the most endlessly wonderful and absorbing spectacle, which demands all our attention. If that is not enough to make one leap out of bed, whatever one's age, in the morning, then the need to fight against stupid, cruel, greedy, self-destructive human behaviour can provide just that extra goad of rage and frustration required to ensure that you will find it impossible to pull up the blankets and opt for sleep.

Strong motivation may be the key to maintaining an active lifestyle for as long as possible. But ultimately we all depend on good health. Nancy Tennant, who died this year aged 105, had a simple formula to account for her longevity: a hearty appetite and an interest in other people. She particularly enjoyed entertaining children who, in turn, were fascinated by her amazing age and sprightliness. There is not much you can do if you lose your appetite, but it is perfectly possible to train yourself to be more interested in other people than in oneself. She was fortunate in that it was as natural to her to have fun playing with children as to enjoy eating a good meal. It is hard to think of a better way of spending one's old age.

Like money, good health is not enough in itself to ensure happiness – but it certainly is the most indispensable ingredient for an active old age. I was stopped dead (or very nearly dead) in my tracks by a heart bypass. In the unreal half-world of hospital, all bets are off. The walls of the ward become the edges of the universe, and the business of survival is totally preoccupying. But if you make it and emerge to start again, the odds are that your appetite for life will be sharpened. Getting extra time makes you more appreciative of what is on offer and, with any luck, you will have more energy to help you enjoy it.

JEFFREY SMART
A DIRTY CON TRICK

WE WERE told of the rewards of old age: the dignity, the wisdom.

This was a dirty con trick. There are no rewards. The dignity is more about walking very carefully to avoid tripping up and the consequent new hip job.

Wisdom? Oldies seem sillier than many youngies.

Perhaps one consolation: we are all ten years younger these days, thanks to medical science, surgery, diet and vitamin additions.

Biologically, I'm eighty-three – but I fancy I'm more like an over-matured seventy-three.

Dan Somerville
Keeping Going

BOOKS have been written on how to slow down the inexorable clock: take up a hobby, do something creative, learn a foreign language, keep in touch with your friends. It's like doing gym exercises in your bedroom: hard work, but perhaps it's worth it. It's puritanical. But does the puritan enjoy life? Can you keep young unless you do?

A subject like this forces you to think analytically. But should you? As the song has it: 'Life's a pleasant institution; let us take it as it comes.'

Stop playing tennis when you can't give the other fellow a game, but it's just as important to replace one enthusiasm with another. Remember the terrible graffiti: 'Tomorrow has been cancelled due to lack of interest.' I was once told by someone in the Civil Service Department that his retired people had a habit of dying within seven years. 'You see,' he said, 'their life has been shaped by their work: the semi in Bromley, the garden kept neat at weekends. And now they're at home all day. Their wives are busier than ever, but their own lives have no significance.'

My great-aunt, Edith Somerville, the authoress, filled her long life with enthusiasms. She believed she could succeed at whatever she set her hand to: writing, painting, playing the organ, hunting foxes, gardening, learning Irish. She must be the only Master of Fox Hounds to have produced a musical comedy (with local talent). In her late seventies she sat up all night with two sick dogs, noting the times and quantities of food administered, starting with milk and chicken and ending with castor oil, laudanum and RIP. I never thought of her as old, though one hip was crippled solid by arthritis.

She never visited the past, except to make money out of it (she wrote two books of memoirs). Certainly, to spend much time there seems to hasten the ageing process. The feebly flapping whale, washed up on the beach of today, remembers all too clearly the oceans of yesterday in which he spouted and swam. The trouble is, spouting is all he can do now, and too much spouting can bring on the final agent in the ageing process – loneliness. From then on, the slide accelerates.

These days we have less excuse than ever for visiting the past. The present is so much better: better cars, better telephones, (remember how long it used to take to ring the Continent?) central heating everywhere, cigarettes nowhere, clean air, cleaner rivers, no dirty steam trains. I feel younger already!

ALYSON SPOONER
HELP!

I AM working very hard at trying to become like the sister who loved pink in *The Grass Harp* by Truman Capote. But I have a sneaking feeling that I am much more like her sister, watching the clock to make sure that everyone does everything on time – *help!!*

JAMES SPOONER

CRUSTINESS

I READ that Dutch researchers claim: 'a positive attitude lengthens one's life span.' What rubbish. I am relieved that someone has also said: 'a clear link between cheerfulness and health is hard to establish.'

I thrive on getting increasingly crusty: with myself, my knees, stiffness and lack of nimbleness – and with the world around me. I rather enjoy being a depressive: though not at three in the morning when the whole picture does seem bleak – but this may, of course, be the effect of over-lavish consumption the night before.

'Late Youth' Bah! I want none of that. We are all living too long – pills morning and night, pacemakers, new hips, bypasses; prostate problems, STENTs *et al.* I do not worry about death – in the abstract – though, no doubt, if faced with an assassin about to shoot me, I would be terrified.

I have not had a stroke – yet – but my inner thoughts get more and more cantankerous. Religion, never a favourite, has become a constant windmill to tilt against. Most of my adult life has been overshadowed by ghastly near-religious dogma of extreme right or extreme left. One hoped in the 1990s that, by the millennium, this would have gone for good. Not a bit. We now have the wretched Muslim fundamentalists and, horror of horrors, Christian fundamentalists across the United States of America.

I detest religious organizations, political correctness, Christmas, planning officers, petty and not-so-petty bureaucrats and airports. All this keeps me going very happily.

So – I can sit back and enjoy:

Music – opera; even more chamber music and lieder; the lovely Royal Academy of Music with its brave, optimistic young people.

Films – thanks to my daughter I have returned to the screen: *Station Agent*, *Fog of War*, *Fahrenheit 9/11*, *The Weeping Camel*, *Before Sunset* and *Before Sunrise*, these last two best seen in that reverse order, and many others.

The Wonderful English Countryside – during this unpromising last summer we made various trips: Northumberland and Yorkshire, houses and gardens; Norfolk coast, children and grandchildren; a son in Devon; a daughter at Lepe on the Solent. All beautiful and each in gorgeous weather.

One's Family – long suffering – and lovely friends and colleagues. So I have nothing, but nothing, to complain about.

I can raise a glass of Pinot Grigio and fume happily at the bloodiness of the world: bloody Blair, bloody Bush, bloody Putin, bloody Sharon, bloody knees, bloody HEFC, bloody Arts Council, bloody Chirac, bloody Berlusconi and bloody Brussels.

But then one remembers crusty old Beethoven with his uplifting, optimistic Triple Concerto; the last movement of the Ninth; the second act of *Fidelio*, which we saw magnificently performed in the Wiener Staatsoper in November, and realizes there *is* Hope and Joy and Freedom – and Alyson. Gosh! I am lucky. Amen.

John Stefanidis
I Am But Thirty

Whereas I benefit from the wisdom of my maturity, I cannot write about getting older, as in my heart I am but thirty.

DAVID TANG
FILIAL PIETY

WE CHINESE, taught by Confucius, strongly believe in filial piety. The idea is that our children should look after us as we grow old. This must also mean that having more children will procure more filial piety. That is why Chinese men up to the generation of my great-grandfather augmented their wives with lots of concubines. This increased the possibility of more and more children and, therefore, more and more filial piety.

So, my great-grandfather took five concubines after his wife. He then built a house with six storeys and placed his wife on the ground floor, then each of his concubines on a floor above, leaving the penthouse for himself. He would work through the week by ascension, staying with his wife first and then with one concubine on each floor, ending on Sunday by himself, resting on top of the building. He obviously knew what he was doing as he had a great time growing old, pampered by his enlarged family. His son, my grandfather, did more or less the same, except that he was more modest with only three concubines but scattered them round the city because he didn't want them to gossip all day.

My father could not, however, enjoy concubines, for polygamy became illegal in Hong Kong and concubines were regarded as wives. I certainly have not been able to deviate from monogamy – which I thought, before I learned English properly, was a kind of wood.

219

The whole point of having as many concubines as possible is to ensure the best way of living in old age. There would not only be concubines to look after us but all their children too; my children and filial piety would flow with our ageing.

I don't know how, having just reached fifty, I can depend on concubines, as I have not been allowed any by my English wife. It's most unfortunate, and she herself is the loser, as my concubines' children would have been bound to respect her as my wife, and she would have been looked after, because of her seniority as a wife, by all the other concubines and their children. But somehow, Lucy, my wife, is not persuaded, even if I remind her that in *As You Like It*, the Bard wrote: 'Though I look old, yet I am strong and lusty.' Too bad!

ANNE TREE

I'M SEVENTY-EIGHT AND LOVING IT

I'M seventy-eight and loving it. I move very slowly on crutches and use my knees as an excuse for bad behaviour, playing the disabled card for all it's worth. My sister, who's very deaf, does the same and turns off her hearing aid whenever she's bored.

Gardening is one of my passions, and I now have a flowerbed known as 'Handicap Corner'. It's raised to one metre high, is ten metres long and one metre wide. I sit on a chair to garden.

My bedroom is on the ground floor, has a panic button and a television set. No mirror. I don't have mirrors anywhere. My stepmother-in-law, Marietta Tree, once asked me why I didn't have a facelift, and I answered, quoting Hilaire Belloc:

> My face, I'm behind it
> Therefore I don't mind it.
> It's the people in front get the jar.

My power shower is too powerful to stand up in. It would knock me over, so I sit down. There's a little step down into a whirlpool: a monsoon. I sit on a wooden seat that is warm to the touch. It has a proper drain. Everything, including my hair, gets soaked. I don't mind this and have a loathing of shower-caps. It amounts to a phobia. I hate the touch. A cotton one might be all right. It's the rubber I can't bear.

I travel constantly and adore it. I make a huge fuss at airports, and if I'm lucky I get put into 'Serenity Corner'. Oddly enough the 'Serenity' lavatory is on the floor below, so I lose my street cred when I walk down a flight. Lavatories aren't always easy to get off, so I travel with a rubber ring and often bounce into the air.

I did once have St Vitus Dance. Not only my legs but also my entire body jumped about. I heard people shouting 'Better strap her down' and screamed to the doctors that I was St Vitus, but none of them had ever heard of him. When I got home I copied out a brief description of him from the *Oxford Book of Saints* and sent it to them.

I've always been obsessed with politics; since earliest consciousness I've been a committed Tory wet. At the age of five I was allowed to lunch downstairs and would say to my father, then Undersecretary for India: 'I'm telling you, Daddy, Baldwin's no good'.

Politics are still a passionate and ecstatic joy. I'm obsessed. If there's a big issue, I speak to my sister about it three times a day on the telephone – to my brother, until his recent death, twice a day. It has always been meat and drink to all three of us.

If, as I am, you are lucky enough not to be afraid of death and quite expect to fall down dead each day, you are free to do everything you like best: drink, chat, stay up late. There's no possible reason not to have the best possible time every day. Being behind a Zimmer frame makes no difference whatsoever.

I adore restaurants. I'd like to die having lunch at Wilton's with Rupert Loewenstein.

GILLY WARRENDER
'BE YOUR AGE!'

'OH, BE your age!' How many times have those words been thrown at us? But what age is suggested? I suppose we are meant to be more grown-up – less silly.

All right – but if someone should say that to me, as a seventy-three-year-old, I'm not sure I would want to comply. I have always thought that seventy or more is old – but I don't feel old (except when I look in the mirror). I do not want to behave old. What age would I prefer to be? Which period in my life did I most enjoy?

I look back on my thirties with pleasure and nostalgia, but I dreaded reaching my thirtieth birthday. It seemed to mark the end of youth and the beginning of descent into middle age. I have a great friend who is twenty-one days older than me and we came up with the idea that we give a joint birthday party to celebrate – or rather to mourn the depressing event. All our friends would be asked to come dressed in black. The party never got beyond the planning stage. If others shared this feeling, I bet they were all female. I think it was Oscar Wilde who said that the five longest years of a woman's life were between twenty-nine and thirty.

After taking the plunge into my forties, I enjoyed myself. My shyness receded. My confidence grew, and although I invested in more face creams and tried to eat fewer chocolate éclairs, I had a good time and would have liked to 'be my age'. I initiated a bargain with my younger daughter that I would give up smoking if she would. She married, went on smoking, became pregnant and stopped smoking. Of course, she challenged me to stop too. Eventually I did with the help of a hypnotist – but by this time I was well into my fifties. This was a definite minus with which to start the decade. I may have become healthier – certainly fatter – but driving or playing bridge was never to be the same without that lovely tobacco.

I remember my fifties without much enthusiasm. Nothing particular comes to mind – I was indisputably middle-aged and menopausal, and I don't think I want to be that age again. Reaching my sixties was not nearly as bad as I had feared. Lots of new hobbies and enthusiasms. We moved house and enjoyed new friends and new gardening. I didn't at all mind 'being my age' during those years. Charming grandsons growing up, then the addition of an Italian daughter-in-law, followed by an enchanting half-Italian granddaughter. Yes. I liked 'being my age' in my sixties.

Now I am in my seventies, and I reserve judgement on how much I do and shall enjoy it. I am all too conscious of that dreaded 'winged chariot'. My beloved husband died, closely followed by our adored Columbus in her ninety-eighth dog year. More and more friends are dropping off their perches, and if I let myself brood, the future looks bleak.

But enough of that – I have wonderful children and grandchildren and lots of ideas of what I want to do: travel to places I do not yet know, indulge myself at cookery courses in France and Italy, find hidden talent as an artist (I am always an optimist) and of course, arrange an introduction to a new dog: not quite yet – but soon. I hope I will be able to enjoy my progression into my eighties without remotely 'being my age'.

MY COUSIN RACHEL

IT IS hardly surprising if, for those who can remember her, Cousin Rachel was always old. Her father fought in the Crimean War, and her brother, Rene – pronounced 'Rainy' – won a Victoria Cross at Omdurman. She herself had been engaged to Freddie Roberts, son of the famous field marshal of that name, and Freddie, like Rainy, was killed in the Boer War.

A small photograph of Freddie in a little silver frame sat on Rachel's desk to her dying day. You can imagine what he looked like: narrow face, parting, pencil moustache – just like Rainy. Even in her nineties, she would, before sitting down at her desk, move the photograph a fraction of an inch to the right or to the left and say, 'Freddie Roberts, dearie.' Occasionally she would add: 'If I could go off the rails now, I would. Oh lor, dearie…'

Upstairs in the Dorset manor house she had built with her sister, Kathleen, in 1914 – 'mock Elizabethan, dearie' – was Kathleen's bedroom. It had remained untouched since her death in the early thirties: a shrine to sibling love. Not far away in a peaceful country churchyard near the beautiful Queen Anne house that Rachel had inherited from her mother lay the remains not only of Kathleen and Rainy but also of Rachel's parents and of her younger sister, Blanche, who died in the 1890s, aged twenty-one, of cholera in India. Even Willoughby, the last Viscount Frankfort de Montmorency, is there, despised as he was by his sisters for having married beneath his station – and to a divorced woman at that. A marble angel spreads its wings over each one of them. Only Rachel has a humbler headstone.

For a child, Rachel's house held the enchantment of an Aladdin's cave, crowded as it was with sentimental pictures of Jesus among the bluebells, musical boxes and mah-jong sets and every kind of ornament – 'dingbats, dearie' – from Benares brass monkeys and ivory elephants to the delicate, prancing china horses that adorned her dining-room table. 'We bagged them,' she'd say, as she moved them gently from their allotted places, 'from the Summer Palace'.

Rachel's maternal grandfather, Field Marshal Sir John Michel, had indeed been rewarded for the 'zeal, skill and intrepidity' with which his division burned down the Summer Palace during the Occupation of Peking in 1860: something of which she was very proud.

In the oak panelled hall hung a chalk drawing of Rachel as a young woman. Her hair and eyes were dark, her profile fearsome even then, with a strong, hooked nose, determined chin and thin, set lips. 'I was rather lovely, dearie,' she often said. But my grandfather always used to maintain that, 'Freddie Roberts had a *demmed* lucky escape'.

If only we had had the sense to ask cousin Rachel about the past, about her life as a young woman with her soldier father in Alexandria or in Bengal, what a lot she might have been able to tell us. She must also have had interesting memories of her grandparents, even of the hero who burned down the Summer Palace.

The name de Montmorency was adopted by the Irish family of Mount Morris some time during the early years of the nineteenth century and was, according to *The Complete Peerage,* the biggest cock and bull story ever to be foisted upon the English aristocracy. This didn't prevent Rachel from making frequent references to 'our French cousins, dearie'. So, one way and another, she built for herself a quite unnecessary fantasy world of grandeur, developing an equally grand manner to go with it, snorting and waving a dismissive, bejewelled hand in the direction of her long-suffering Switzer Deutsch maid whom she addressed in incomprehensible French. Josephine replied in a mixture of pidgin French and excellent English as she helped Madam apply her rouge. 'I *was* rather lovely, dearie.'

And if anyone dared so much as to smile at Rachel's malapropisms, they were rewarded with a haughty look of such utter contempt that even when, with regard to a bothy, she announced: 'I'm building a brothel for the gardeners,' not a muscle was seen to move on anyone's face.

What was it then that kept Rachel going for so long? Surely not the pre-war Rover with green leather seats that used to boil over on every hill as she drove to the coast for a lobster tea. She would urge it on with a forward lurch of her body as she gripped the steering wheel, talking to it all the while as if it were an obstinate horse. But perhaps she treated herself rather as she treated the car, expecting it to go on forever, reluctant to believe that its engine was wearing out.

She enjoyed changing her will – malice was not unknown to her – and quarrelling with her relations, rearranging her dingbats, saving money, being given things like plums and crab apples, and she enjoyed playing cards – canasta was her game. She played it with unparallel intensity. Heedless of the tender age of her opponent, she played to win. And not just to win, but to wipe the floor with whatever ten-year-old child she may have happened upon as a playmate. Yet children loved her because she shared so many of their pleasures and their attitudes, and unlike other grownups she never tired of their endless prattle. All of these things must have helped to keep her going.

But, above all, Rachel was fearless and, were a marble angel to spread its wings over her grave, it would be the angel of courage for, as she was wont to say: 'We'd better bat on, dearie'.

SOPHY WEATHERALL
HOW TO DEAL WITH THE CADAVER

FOR me, the fiftieth birthday definitely seemed to be the turning point – when the slow but relentless senior maturing process began. Luckily technology in the shape of opticians, dentists and others smoothed the way from then on.

Having made a will and dealt, as far as possible, with potential tax problems in order to leave things as tidy and simple as possible for those left in charge, I was faced with the question as to whether to give precise, vague or no instruction whatever as to how to deal with the cadaver. To me, death is final and not at all frightening. I have no belief of any kind in any afterlife and will be very interested if I find that I am proved wrong. Being not only Scottish but also having grown up in the early 1940s when life was pretty frugal, I dislike any form of waste, so I have arranged for my corpse to go to the Department of Anatomy at Edinburgh University in the hope that some medical student may learn something from it. In their letter of acceptance the Department did point out that there were a few unpleasant diseases that would render a body unwelcome. They also mentioned that they close over Bank Holidays and would be unable to receive any donations at that time. I am not sure if the same rules apply to undertakers and/or gravediggers, but *do* watch the calendar if you are really getting on.

My husband has just passed his eightieth birthday, and my favourite of his cards said: 'To a man who has everything going for him. Eyes going, teeth going, hearing going...'

Top tip for coping with ageing husbands or similar: if you do not fancy installing a urinal, invest in several towelling 'pedestal' mats. It seems the aim deteriorates, and the drips proliferate.

NATALIE WHEEN
TOO OLD?

IT WAS the chainsaw that did it. I couldn't see what was so funny in my search for a lady-sized chainsaw, but the mirth seemed to be universal. 'You? Cutting the trees?' (They meant pruning.) They weren't amazed at the fair(ish), fat and fifty-something bit, or even the wielding the chainsaw. It was the climbing trees to wield the said saw that finished them.

Now, I see nothing strange in cutting trees. In fact, I've been cutting trees all my life. Well, mentally at least – because I have to admit that there has been something of a gap in the last few decades living in London when to climb a tree would have invited instant arrest. But I've always sized them up for tree-climbing qualities: toeholds, well spaced branches and, of course, the ultimate goal from which to spy out the surroundings, to scan the far horizon (so to speak).

But there's never really been the right moment to do something about it until olive trees came into my life. With olive trees, you positively *have* to climb them, going for that last, fattest, plum-sized olive out of reach from the ground, to thwack at the elusive harvest on the topmost branches and, of course, to prune. Some locals take the easy way, amputating the bother by simply cutting out the main trunk, but I prefer to be obsessive about shape and light and all that English stuff which only labels us mad in other parts of the world.

It is cheating a little with olive trees: I must be scrupulously honest. It's not so much climbing up, but stepping out onto the branches, still satisfyingly vertiginous when looking down on the terrace below and perfectly high enough to get back to those delicious early fantasies of sailing off on a pirate ship, Jolly Roger stiff in the breeze, and making the enemy walk the plank. I used to spend hours captaining the ship in the big old tree in the kitchen garden, safe – for a few hours, I always prayed – from Mama's inevitable screaming hysteria predicting any amount of gruesome ends if I persisted in such dangerous games, unsupervised. She always dragged me away. I always went back at the next opportunity. It was the best place in the world for escape.

I saw the old tree not so long ago. Someone's done terrible things to it, but it's still there. So am I. Mama isn't. Come to think of it, the best thing really about being this old is that she is no longer with us. Bliss that the telephone no longer transmits that terrible complaining whine: 'Mum here…' I can't remember how many times she was made to walk the plank in my scheme of things. And certain other members of the family.

They've nearly all gone actually, and the old saying couldn't be truer about choosing your friends because you're stuck with the family. It's bliss being an orphan.

Which takes me back to the trees. Perhaps I should thank the old bat for instilling such a passion for them – if she hadn't shrieked maybe it would have just been a passing fancy. As it is, I shall probably fall out of one sooner or later. What a way to go!

MARTIN WILKINSON

THE BLOCK OF FROZEN TIME

MUSIC can freeze time. Listen to a piece of music that you loved years ago, and you can go back through the block of frozen time to touch the other side, remerging now as you were then. Many have reported this phenomenon: that music keeps them young, makes them feel sixteen again and rolls back the years – the clustering of apocryphal sayings around it is a sure sign of universal experience. But in order to come to terms with time, it first has to be measured, whether in the workings of the processes of decay all around and in us or in the demarcation of events. Music is measured by its own internal time. It changes according to the moods of its listeners, its performers and its composers. It creates tribal allegiances on the basis of its own construction and the times with which it is associated. Music, in this tribal aspect, can unfortunately also be used to oppress and disorientate the stranger, the member of the other tribe – perhaps the 'grey tribe' as we older people are beginning to be called: we members of that strange musical tribe wandering in the wastes of irrelevance to which we seem to have been banished by the miasmas of youth culture and faction. The shock of the new can redeem as well as repel; but how can we defend ourselves against the onslaught of garage, rap, dissonance, atonal constructions, *musique concrète*...whatever doesn't get us through the night? We have probably all felt at one time or another like Sir Thomas Beecham who, when someone asked him in his old age if he had come across any Stockhausen, replied: 'I think I might have trod in some on my way over here.' But *pace* Stockhausen and Beecham, the peaceful remedy and the answer lie where the question started: in us. Like music itself, it has to do with scale. Logically, it's absurd to devalue anything simply on the basis of its relative size. Music can be seen as a vast landscape. If we don't like something musical, it simply means that it is a very small part of our musical world, to be respected nonetheless. We can work with the bits of music we like to improve our understanding of them and ourselves through them. Music's power to rejuvenate us will then constantly reinvent and renew itself. Even those pieces that seem to sink an ice pick into our skulls will become benign, if small, parts of the musical landscape. When the power of music – old or new – carries us away, everyone, in the depths of their soul, becomes a listener, a performer and a composer. Personally, I take an almost musical consolation from walking at night while I can still do it. A road or track is best for obvious reasons, and while urban landscapes are perennially fascinating, they are dangerous after dark for the silver-haired nowadays. My greatest pleasure is a circular walk around a country village at night, with all the mystery that the night adds to the sight and sounds of sleeping houses, odd lights across fields, cattle sheds and sleeping byres, the night sky, great trees under the moon; my thoughts instantly enter meditation mode. When walking fails, there will be a guitar or piano to sound; and finally I will just listen to the music of the natural world in which, by then, I ought to be able to discern the symphonies that I have been hoping to hear for so long.

VANESSA WILLIAMS ELLIS

I AM WEARING OUT MY BOOTS

FOR twenty years I ran a bookshop in Paddington, but that was another life. My feet wore a hole in the carpet where I sat, and I felt I must get some exercise and fresh air – so I bought a farm.

It seemed to be the perfect way to get the exercise and air that I craved and at the same time to keep my independence and earn a living. I have this fantasy that I am running a prep school or am matron with my hundred and sixty charges, all female, the pregnant ewes. 'Good morning girls, time to get up,' I call brightly as I come round the corner of the lambing shed at six in the morning, feeling completely in control of a hundred and sixty individuals who are tidily penned in and meekly obedient. People say they are the substitutes for the children I never had – maybe, but a hundred and sixty of them and all so meek. The cows are different and fearsome in their size and the brute strength of their necks. The excitement when a calf is born never diminishes. That makes me feel more like a god than a matron. I never had a hamster or goldfish so didn't learn to love animals; it just came upon me – first sheep and then cattle. Sometimes I am responsible for as many as five hundred demanding individuals. They need attention all day in all weathers. Then there is the grass and hedges, the hay and straw and the buildings to see to. This makes it hard to get away – so bang has gone the sort of freedom I thought I wanted. But I do have the freedom to do what I enjoy and never spend the days longing to go home or the weeks longing for the weekends. I plan my day over breakfast, but it never turns out quite right. The sheep break out, or I have a visitor and never catch up and find myself stumbling about in the dark. The dogs don't get fed till late, and a fox gets into the henhouse. When that happened, not long ago, I shut myself into the henhouse with the fox and killed it with a broom handle before racing in to cook dinner for guests – remembering to take the reviving lamb out of the bottom oven before putting the plates in to warm – and the leg of lamb in the top oven.

On other days all goes swimmingly, and I have time for a cocktail at six.

I have been farming for twenty years. Time and the exercise are catching up on me. The carpets are as good as the day we moved in, but I am wearing out my boots and my bones: three pairs of boots a year and frequent visits to my GP for inspection of a painful knee or a locked thumb. He is not very sympathetic, always offering the advice 'use it or lose it', which I find surprisingly reassuring and thank goodness for a licence to carry on. I am no longer independent but harried, chivvied, regulated, recorded and inspected by DEFRA. I suppose I can just about pay my way to the farm gate. But fresh air, lots of it, rain, sun, wind, huge skies, real darkness and stars at night – the valley is beautiful, and I love it. I do have a let-out when it gets too hickish and hodgelike. I hire a minder, get back to my first love, sit in the subfusc gloom of a silent airless library and have the time of my life, cataloguing books and resting my legs.

Alice Windsor Clive
The Delights Of Hunting Don't Fade

ONE of the most annoying things that people can say to me is: 'Are you *still* hunting?'

I started to feel that hunting was an essential part of life in my fifties, when I moved to a thatched cottage half a mile from the boundary of Exmoor National Park with a much-loved chestnut mare, whose head I could see over her stable door from my bedroom window.

As a child I didn't hunt, although I rode endlessly, on my own, on a series of ponies. At that time the lanes were empty. No farmer turned me off his land. The park around our house was unfenced. I went wherever I chose.

The house itself was full of hunting prints and sporting paintings. One in particular I loved: an old codger in a battered top hat, wrinkled breeches and a benign rosy-cheeked face entitled 'The Hero of the Chase'. He had owned a pack in Surrey and was an ancestor of mine.

I read *The Irish RM* and *Memoirs of a Foxhunting Man* avidly. Then at fourteen I went off to a convent school, and my pony was sold.

Years later, with four small children and a house on the edge of London, I longed for an escape from domesticity.

Once a week I climbed into hunting gear (including stock) and drove to Berkshire, hoping to get back in one piece in time to put the children to bed.

237

I knew nothing at all about the etiquette of the hunting field and once brought a master down by careering in front of him at a jump: odd that I wasn't sent home. I fell off often but only once broke my collarbone.

Later still we moved to Somerset, acquired ponies and more horses, and the children began to hunt. We learned by our mistakes, made friends, had fun. I occasionally ventured out to Exmoor to hunt with the Devon and Somerset, following Diana Scott scrambling up and down steep banks, fording torrents, negotiating bogs.

After I had settled into the cottage the delights of hunting as an older woman began. No more dashing back to pick up children from school and feed large numbers.

The exquisite pleasure of a hot bath, a glass of whisky, bacon and eggs and a snooze is a solitary one. Through old friends I made new ones and began to fit together the jigsaw of woods, rivers, hidden places that is Exmoor, although I much prefer to have someone born and bred locally to act as pilot.

Hunting together is a key that unlocks friendship with shy and unlikely people. There is little ageism. Most of the leading figures are of mature years. A fine example locally are the Lloyd twins; they are round about the age of eighty and have many pins and plastic hips between them, but to see them cracking into a howling gale, eyes sparkling with excitement, old bowlers tipped forward, is to see two school boys.

The archetypal image of the hunting lady of a certain age is plum-voiced, burgundy-faced, moustachioed and terrifying. I had a son-in-law – Will Self – who coined the phrase 'barbed-wire eater'.

My heroine of the chase (who used to fly across Leicestershire side-saddle) has a rose-petal skin and the warmest heart of all. Her surgeon refused to hammer her leg together if she continued to ride to hounds; now, at nearly eighty, she rides, still side-saddle, in the early mornings when not at the races or picking up at a shoot.

Another cliché is that hunting people never read anything but

Horse and Hound. How about my professor friend, Sir Raymond Carr? At over eighty, he charges up to unknown ladies during a dull moment and bellows at them: 'Who was the better rider? Tolstoy or Turgenev?' Though surprised, the ladies certainly answer back.

Hunting is a haven for old eccentrics – one of the finest being my friend Charles Parker (now alas moved to Ireland): famous as terrier-man and harbourer, superb version of tunnel vision, having no place in his life for a house, possessions or a family. Luckily when the physical work became tricky he took up garden design with equal ferocity; but hunting made him.

I don't believe there is another sport that fosters such enthusiasm and talent and keeps people so young.

Of course, there are hunting pleasures when you are young – competitiveness and flirtations and cutting a dash – but the delights don't fade as you sit on top of a hill and watch the thrusters roaring off in the wrong direction. It's just more relaxed.

PS When I was writing the above the future of hunting was in limbo; there was huge speculation, but nothing was certain. Now it is fatally clear that by the time this is in print it will take another act of parliament to remove the ban. All we can do is protest, ridicule and 'test' the new law, and we are in for a long battle of wits and nerve. My friends are full of determination.

OLD AGE HAS TAKEN ME BY SURPRISE

OLD age has taken me by surprise. I find that I think about it too much – even wonder when it officially begins; seventy-five seems right as a rule of thumb. What is it that one is really thinking about though? Perhaps it's death rather than old age. We shouldn't be that much frightened by death. It probably has an anticlimactic side to it, given that everyone who has lived has experienced it – or will.

The chance of another life seems less and less likely: at least of another life with any awareness of a connection to the present one. So, reincarnation must be a non-starter, if one life has no link with a possible other: first me, then a rat in a Neapolitan museum or whatever. Meaningless.

There used to be some comfort to be gained from the idea that we might in this life be mere emanations from something far greater – like sparks out of a fire. But the physicists come closer and closer to convincing me that life started by chance contacts as a result of (but long after) a 'singularity' or 'Big Bang'. So that comfort has gone – and if we are faced with oblivion, the terms of life seem unfair and the 'goodbyes' astonishingly ruthless.

Leonard Woolf called his post-sixty autobiography *Downhill all the Way*. But to most of us it feels more like uphill.

Everyone is confronted by different symptoms of old age in varying degrees – forgetting names and deafness. I am seriously deaf, anyway, as a result both of the army and heredity: I get a pension. Being deaf is tiring, always sitting on the edge of the chair, hesitant to meet new people. National Health hearing aids are the most powerful. Sleeping is not as easy as it used to be, but that is unimportant. Wakefulness provides an opportunity to read, which often acts as a soporific.

When I was fifty-eight I woke one morning with blurred vision in one eye and went to the doctor for the first time in twenty-five years. A grey-haired lady, shortly to retire, took my blood pressure, looked at me through her glasses in a rather surprised way, and said: 'It is astronomically high.' My father died suddenly from a stroke aged fifty-four, so I decided to take things easy from there on; luckily this coincided with my business having been bought out. But things were made difficult by a second divorce a few years later.

There are some compensations now. I feel I'm looking on from the outside: a bit more objective. Less prejudiced perhaps. Life is still enjoyable: certainly travel and having my films developed afterwards. I don't print them myself anymore – too much effort. Once I organized an art exhibition and included dozens of my own photographs. Looking at painting and architecture becomes more enjoyable with experience. Lucky not to be blind – I don't think I could manage that. Where I live I can walk for miles in every direction and still do – may even stupidly go skiing once more.

What happens in the world is no less fascinating. TV documentaries and history, football and cricket are entertaining, and Ceefax is useful. The mere idea of 'Reality TV' is revolting.

Six years ago I had a heart bypass but didn't think I was going to die. Perhaps I was more optimistic than the situation justified. A third of people apparently get brain damaged after my particular operation, but I haven't noticed much difference. Lots of aspirin helps to thin the blood, but try not to cut yourself.

Euthanasia might be a good idea, provided the patient has a say. No one wants a doctor announcing: 'We'll give him until the end of the week!' The thought of a retirement home – or whatever – is a bit alarming. But we should be prepared for it. What percentage of us nowadays ends up in one?

Old age is like a narrow one-way street with the potholes getting worse as you drive down it. It is better to keep going if we can – until we meet that b****r with a scythe in his hand coming the other way.

PEREGRINE WORSTHORNE

OLD AGE

THE only thing that makes old age seem tolerable is the thought of the alternative. I cannot remember who said that first, but it is usually quoted as a clinching argument to the proposition that the old should feel lucky to be still alive. Which is true, of course. We are lucky to be still alive, but only in the same way as a lifer in prison is lucky to have escaped hanging – in other words, not really lucky at all in any sensible use of the word. No, the reality is that old age is perfectly horrible, and those oldsters who write otherwise have either not yet experienced old age – i.e. not yet experienced any serious failure of mental or physical powers – or are merely whistling in the dark – however understandably – to keep their spirits up.

Mostly in the former category, I would suppose, since I recall writing a piece twenty years ago, when I was in my sixties, extolling the pleasures of old age: the license it bestowed on one to be bad-tempered and rude, to demand respect for merely having a head full of grey hairs, to laze around all day reading a novel and so on and suchlike. Old age, in other words, was one long holiday. Unfortunately, that is only one phase of old age: the health phase; the phoney phase. For, of course, declining physical and mental powers are the defining characteristics of old age, and if that curse has not yet descended, you really cannot be expected to write knowledgeably about old age, just as someone crippled at birth cannot be expected to write knowledgeably about the joys of youth.

I know better now. Old age involves 'letting go'. It is an extraordinarily painful process, and no one wants to dwell on the reality of what it is they are preparing to renounce forever. Hence all that whistling in the dark, all that self-deluding talk about keeping young in spirit, making new friends, developing fresh interests and enthusiasms, keeping up with the times etc. Unquestionably, this is better than moaning but dangerously misleading if anyone should confuse a bravura performance for the real thing. The closer one gets to the day of judgement, the less wise it is to risk being caught cheerful and smiling, as if exuding confidence about what that judgement is likely to be. Complacency is to be avoided at all stages in your life and never more so that at the last call.

I HAVE ENTERED A CALMER SEA

I CELEBRATED my sixtieth birthday with a party nearly two years ago. My children had all grown up: two of them married with five children between them. Simon and I had been together for nearly thirty years. I found myself with the same kind of confidence I had as a child; this had been missing for a large part of my adult life. It seemed like a good reason for a party.

Since then I have been having a love affair with a tiny shepherd's cottage on the Firle estate in Sussex. For me, it is a magical place. Many interesting, creative people have been drawn to the area. The atmosphere has inspired me to read, write, dream and paint. Sometimes after hours at the kitchen table, totally absorbed in painting, my muse, Leafy – a black and white whippet who appears in many of my pictures – takes me out onto the Downs.

As a London child, I used to stay with my grandparents at Oare in Wiltshire. I remember the adventure of getting up early and walking through several fields on my own to help milk the cows. What I loved was the intimacy of pressing my head against their warm bodies and squeezing milk from their bursting udders into the pails. Their grassy breath steamed in the cold morning air. I swam naked in the swimming pool that my grandfather had built in the 1930s.He told me he could stand in the middle of the pool with his top hat reaching the surface of the water.

I was a confident, rebellious and independent child and lived very much in my own world. The grownups I knew never talked about their feelings, nor could I communicate mine to them. So when I read *The Unquiet Grave,* I was deeply touched when I found out that Cyril Connolly, one of my mother's closest friends, was able to write so openly about his angst and other feelings. I also encountered Buddha's teaching: know thyself. Those discoveries were to be important to me throughout my life. As a young woman, I was tossed around on stormy seas of love, separations and depression.

After a few years of therapy, I became a therapist. Thirty years on, I have entered a calmer sea. I am a confident, independent and rebellious granny.

I think these lines from T. S. Eliot's *Little Gidding* sum up where I am on my journey:

> We shall not cease from exploration
> At the end of our exploring
> Will be to arrive where we started
> And know the place for the first time.

ABOUT THE CONTRIBUTORS

Elizabeth Ashcombe: Lady Ashcombe. Stunning beauty. Born 1942. Family from Charlottesville and Mississippi. Educated New York. Married Mark Dent-Brocklehurst 1962. Mark died in 1972, whereupon Elizabeth inherited sole responsibility of running and restoring Sudeley Castle. She has done this hugely successfully. A patron of the Cheltenham Arts Festival, qualified as a NLP practitioner, was president of the Environmental Medicine Foundation for five years. Currently writing a book on twentieth-century Sudeley and her experiences there. Soon to retire after thirty-five years of running it and will hand over to her children, Henry and Mollie, and their families. In 1979 she married Harry, Lord Ashcombe.

Sir Jack Baer: Born 1924. Educated Bryanston, Slade School of Fine Art, University College London. Served in RAF 1942-1946. Independent fine art consultant. Proprietor, Hazlitt Gallery 1948-1973. On every known committee connected with fine art in the country, including being a member of the Reviewing Committee on Export of Works of Art and a trustee of the *Burlington Magazine.* He has published numerous exhibition catalogues and articles. Highly skilled at the drawing board.

Christopher Balfour: Lived between England and Peru until the age of twelve. Educated at Ampleforth, at the Sorbonne in Paris and at

Oxford, where he made real friends who remain his best friends to this day. Worked as a merchant banker at Hambro's until 1995 when he was recruited to be the European chairman of Christie's until he retired in 2001. From 2001 onwards: doing his best to retain his marbles.

Tessa Baring CBE: Born 1937. Educated Cheltenham Ladies College. Sociologist. Member of the National Lottery Charities Board. Charity Commissioner. Has been chairman of Barnado's. Currently chairman of the Baring Foundation. Awarded CBE for services to the Voluntary Section. Incredibly infectious laugh. Godmother to Silvy Weatherall, one of the daughters of the editor.

David Batterham: Second-hand bookseller specializing in books that can be enjoyed without having to be read: caricature, trade catalogues, fashion magazines, ornament, architecture and textiles, picture books.

Carole Blake: Has worked in publishing for forty-one years. In 1977, started her own literary agency, which merged with Julian Friedmann's agency to become Blake Friedmann in 1983. Past president of the Association of Authors' Agents, past chairman of the Society of Bookmen and currently chairman of the book trade charity, Book Trade Benevolent Society. Her book *From Pitch To Publication* (Macmillan, 1999) is currently in its eighth printing. Writes a regular 'Agent's Diary' for *Mslexia* magazine.

Anthony Blond: Born 1928. In 1952 left family firm, which made underwear for Marks and Spencer, to start his own literary agency. He subsequently created three public businesses; guaranteed *Private Eye*'s overdraft; initiated a literary agency in Japan and a radio station in Manchester. Stood for parliament. Author of several books and has recently published a novel *Family Business*. Having owned houses as far-flung as Sri Lanka, Corfu, New York and Islington, now lives in France with second wife and second son.

John Bowes Lyon: Born in 1942. Educated at Ampleforth. A Knight of Malta. Worked for Sotheby's for many years and is an expert in all forms of works of art. Recently took the editor and her friend, Anne, on a tour of Paris, which was totally enlightening. The pinnacle: a visit to a famous taxidermist in rue du Bac.

Arabella Boxer: Lady Arabella Stuart. Half-Scottish and half-American, lived in the north of Scotland as a child, then in London, making frequent visits to see her grandparents in the USA. Started writing for *Vogue* in 1965 and was their regular food writer for seventeen years. Has published fourteen cookery books and won several awards for food writing: Glenfiddich, Andre Simon, etc. Was married for twenty-four years to Mark Boxer, editor and cartoonist. She has two children and three grandchildren, is now retired and lives in London.

Melvyn Bragg: Lord Bragg of Wigton. Born 1939. Educated Wigton Grammar and Wadham College, Oxford. Writer. Presenter and editor of *The South Bank Show* for ITV since 1978. Controller of Arts, London Weekend Television since 1990. Innumerable fellowships; publications, awards and screenplays. Likes walking and reading.

Harriet Bridgeman: Viscountess Bridgeman. Executive editor, *The Masters* 1996-1998. Editor, *Discovering Antiques* 1968-1970; *Going, Going Gone* series 1973. Founder and managing director, the Bridgeman Art Library since 1971. Company secretary, British Association of Picture Libraries and Agencies. European Woman of the Year Award (Arts Section) 1997. FRSA. Author and editor of several books including *The Encyclopaedia of Victoriana, The Last Word, Society Scandals, Guide to Gardens of Europe*.

Lucy Bridgewater: Talented artist. Born Lucy Bartlett in 1941. Father: Sir Basil Bartlett Bt. actor, *Where the Rainbow Ends*. Mothers:

Mary Malcolm and Nanny. Many schools. Chelsea School of Art. The Royal College of Art. Then the big, wide world.

Georgia Campbell: Lady Colin Campbell was born in St Andrews, Jamaica. She is the author of *Diana in Private*, *The Royal Marriages*, *Lady Colin Campbell's Guide to Being a Modern Lady*, *The Real Diana* and *Empress Bianca* – the latter two titles were published by Arcadia.

Alexander Chancellor: Born in 1940. Educated Eton and Trinity Hall Cambridge. Worked for Reuters 1964-1974 (Rome bureau chief 1968-1973), ITN reporter 1974. Editor, *Spectator* 1975-1984; features editor and subsequently deputy editor, *Sunday Telegraph*, 1984-1986; United States editor, *Independent* 1987-1988; founder-editor, *Independent Magazine*, 1989-2002; editor, Talk of the Town, *New Yorker*, 1993; associate editor, *Sunday Telegraph*, 1994-1995; founder-editor, *Sunday Telegraph Magazine*, 1996; variously columnist for *Sunday Telegraph*, *Daily Express*, *Guardian*, *Daily Telegraph, Slate* magazine, *Saga* magazine. Brother of the editor of this book.

John Paget Chancellor: Born 1927. Early childhood in China. Educated Eton and Cambridge. Served Sixtieth Rifle Brigade. Inner Temple. Provincial journalism. International Insurance. Magazine and part-work publishing (*Knowledge*, *Animals*, *Discovering Art*, *The Masters*, *History Makers*). Book publishing, antiquarian bookselling. Author. Publications include *Darwin*, *Wagner*, *Edward I*, *Audubon*, *Flowers and Fruits of the Bible*. Brother of the editor of this book. Now deals in old books: 65, Ermine Street, Caxton, Cambridgeshire, CB3 8PQ. Tel/Fax: 00 44 (0) 1954 718015 Email: sales@kewbooks-caxton.co.uk Website: www.kewbooks-caxton.co.uk

Robin Chancellor: Born 1921 in London. Educated Eton and Trinity College Cambridge. Worked in munitions factory 1941-1944, then seconded to British Council in Cairo. Rest of working life since war spent in publishing and translating; books and fine art reproductions. World-class ornithologist and dear uncle of the editor of this book. He lives in Northamptonshire.

Sir George Christie CH: Director Glyndebourne Productions Ltd. Chairman 1956-1999. Educated Eton and Cambridge. Has more honours than can possibly mention. Has been cheered along every inch of the way by his life-enhancing wife, Mary.

Thekla Clark: Is not sure when she was born but thinks she is somewhere in her seventies. American by birth, she took Europe by storm as a young beauty and became muse to W. H. Auden. Later wrote a book about their friendship, *Wystan and Chester*, to much acclaim. With her handsome husband, John, ran a photographic printing and publishing firm called La Scala, where they lived (as she still does) in an ancient castle outside Florence. During the troubles in Cambodia, Thekla and John adopted and cared for many orphans. She also wrote a book about this, *Children in Exile*; and the incomparable poet, James Fenton wrote a poem of the same title about the same children.

Maureen Cleave: Born in India in 1934 where her father was in the Indian Army. Read history at St Anne's College, Oxford and became a journalist. Worked for London *Evening Standard*, *Observer* and *Daily Telegraph*. Describes herself as by nature inquisitive and nosey and says that the job suited her perfectly. Her only adventure was being torpedoed in 1940. Lives on the Essex-Suffolk border with her husband and three children.

Isabel Colegate: Much acclaimed author of many best-selling books, including the *Shooting Party*, *The Orlando Trilogy*, *The Summer of the Royal Visit* and, most recently, *A Pelican in the Wilderness*. Lives in a gothic castle with her husband Michael Briggs, Chairman of the Bath

Preservation Society. They have both received honorary degrees from Bath University.

Jilly Cooper OBE: Mrs Leo Cooper. Born 1937. Our greatest comedy writer. Educated Godolphin and Salisbury. Reporter, *Middlesex Independent* 1957-59. Followed by numerous short-lived jobs as account executive, copywriter, publisher's reader, receptionist, puppy-fat model, switchboard wrecker and very temporary typist. Her publications are too numerous to mention, but she has brought great joy into many a life (including that of the editor of this book). Recreations: merrymaking, wild flowers, music and mongrels.

Colin Crewe MC: Born in Addis Ababa in 1922. The emperor became his godfather. Educated Eton College. Went with the Irish Guards to Algiers in 1942. Captured in Anzio and released from camp near Hanover by the Americans in 1945. Married Sally Churchill in 1957 and had three children. Later went in for entrepreneurial 'ventures': Jones (jewellers), ski shops and Night Owls. Ran Reads restaurant in Old Brompton Road before retiring to live in Suffolk in 1990

Polly Devlin, OBE: Broadcaster, writer, conservationist and stunning looker. Her first book, *All Of Us There*, written in 1963, has just been republished as a Virago Modern Classic. She was awarded an OBE for services to literature in 1994.

Deborah Devonshire: The Duchess of Devonshire, DCVO has written many books, including *The House: A Portrait of Chatsworth* and *The Garden at Chatsworth*. She is past president of the Royal Agricultural Association of England and of the Royal Smithfield Club.

Lindy Dufferin: The Marchioness of Dufferin and Ava. Born Lindy Guinness, circa 1940. Painter, botanist, hostess and great supporter of the arts in every form.

Dame Edna Everage (Barry Humphries): Born 1934. Unquestionably a music hall artiste, actor and author of genius. Recreations: kissing, inventing Australia and trailing his coat. Clubs include the Savage in Melbourne.

John Fairbairn: Born 1934. Educated Eton and Cambridge. Chairman of the Esmee Fairbairn Foundation 1988-2003. Trustee and member of many distinguished committees – mainly connected with the arts – Dulwich Picture Gallery, Monteverdi Trust, Museums of Brighton, amongst many others. Much beloved ancestor and friend.

The Honourable Julian Fane: Born in 1927. Has been a Fellow of the Royal Society of Literature since 1974. Author of many highly acclaimed novels, including *Morning*: his first novel that brought him into prominence as a writer. He is married and lives in Sussex.

Desmond Fitzgerald, the Knight of Glin: Runs Glin Castle as a magical country house hotel with his wife, Olda Fitzgerald. Irish art historian who has written on Irish painting, architecture and historic landscape and is currently working on a major book about Irish furniture and carving for Yale University Press. Governor of the National Gallery of Ireland and president of the Irish Georgian society; also serves on various other conservation bodies.

Olda Fitzgerald: Madam Fitzgerald. Has written on Irish painting, architecture and gardens and her books, *Irish Gardens* for Conran Octopus and *Ashford Castle* for the hotel of that name, have recently been published. With her husband, the Knight of Glin, runs Glin Castle as a superb small country house hotel. They also run a dairy farm. She and the knight live at Glin Castle and have three ravishing daughters. Glin Castle has, more than justifiably, been described as 'one of the truly outstanding private houses of the world'. In order to see for yourself, contact: Glin Castle, Glin, Co. Limerick, Ireland. Tel 00 353 (0) 68 34173, Fax; 00 353 (0) 68 34364, Email: knight@iol.ie

Christopher Gibbs: Born 1938. Trustee of J. P. Getty Charitable Trust. Unerring eye for beauty, talent; architecture, furniture and painting. Much loved by all who know him.

Colin Glenconner: Lord Glenconner. Born 1926. Educated Eton and Oxford. Chairman, Mustique Company 1969-87. Now lives in St Lucia and is the uncrowned king of the West Indies. Sparkling wit and generous host.

Jonathan Guinness: Third Baron Moyne. Born 1930. Educated Eton and Oxford. Chairman of the Monday Club 1972-1974. Publications: (with Catherine Guinness) *The House of Mitford, Shoe: The Odyssey of a Sixties Survivor, Requiem for a Family Business*. Yoga devotee.

Maggi Hambling OBE: Born 1945. In her words: 'She is still alive. She's not bad at portraits and has them in the British Museum, the Tate, the National Portrait Gallery *et al*. She was pretty respectable as the National Gallery's first 'Artist in Residence' in 1980 but less so as a moustache-wearing cult TV performer a year or two later. Both the Queen and Mr Jerwood covered her in glory in 1995, since when she's erected sculptures for the likes of Oscar Wilde and Benjamin Britten, which people constantly vandalize and want removed from wherever she puts them'.

Lady Selina Hastings: Author of many highly-acclaimed biographies, including Nancy Mitford, Evelyn Waugh and Rosamond Lehmann. Former literary editor of *Harpers&Queen* and worked as a journalist for the *Daily Telegraph*.

John Haylock: Divides his time between Hove, Japan and Thailand. Author of over twenty books. Arcadia Books has published *Eastern*

Exchange: Memoirs, as well as his novels *Loose Connections*, *Body of Contention* and *Doubtful Partners*. *Sex Gets in the Way*, his latest, is due for publication by Arcadia in 2005.

Drue Heinz: Dame. Best friend to writers everywhere. Greatest encourager and benefactor. Hostess combined with fun-lover (rather rare).

Min Hogg MBE: Fantastically successful editor of *World of Interiors* magazine. Now freelance writer. Very dashing dresser.

Hugh Honour: Born at Eastbourne in 1927. Lives in Italy and is the greatest living art historian: a position he used to share with his companion in life, the late John Fleming. Excellent gardener, cook and extremely fast driver. Among his many publications are *Chinoiserie*, published to world acclaim in 1961; *Companion Guide to Venice* (1965: fourth edition, 1977); with Nikolaus Pevsner and John Fleming: *Penguin Dictionary or Architecture* (1966: fifth edition, 1999); with John Fleming: *A World History of Art* (1982: seventh edition in preparation for 2005).

Elizabeth Jane Howard CBE: Author of twelve highly acclaimed novels, most recently *Falling*, published in 1999. Her *Cazalet Chronicles* have become modern classics and were televised on BBC1. She lives, reads and writes in Suffolk.

Angela Huth: Mrs J. D. Howard-Johnston. Born 1938. Novelist, playwright, part-time journalist, presenter, painter, reporter and tap-dancer. Her many novels include *Landgirls*, *The Trouble with Old Lovers*, and *Wives of the Fishermen*. A feature film was made of *The Landgirls*. Began her writing life on *Queen* magazine in the 1960s, where she met and married Quentin Crewe. Later she went into television as 'the first serious woman reporter in documentaries'. One was *The Englishwoman's Wardrobe*, starring Mrs Thatcher. Her latest book, *Well Remembered Friends*, is a collection of funeral eulogies.

Patricia Huth Ellis: Has had poems published in several magazines, including *Evvoi*, *Second Light*, *The Lady* and local newspapers. Also a recent poem has been published in the *Spectator*. She also arranges poetry presentations in residential homes.

Susanna Johnston: Born 1935. Early years spent in Shanghai where father, Christopher Chancellor, was Reuter correspondent in the Far East. Married Nicholas Johnston, architect, in 1958. Has four daughters and has nine grandchildren. Wrote regular features for the *Tatler*; freelance journalism. Short stories for *Woman* magazine. Books: *Five Rehearsals*, *Collecting*, *The Passionate Pastime*, *The Picnic Papers* (with co-editor Anne Tennant), *Parties: A Literary Companion*.

Charles Keen: Born 1936. Educated Winchester and Oxford. Married Mary Curzon (see Mary Keen) 1962. Poet. Spent most of his life banking, fishing, walking dogs, felling trees. Police record: 1978 drunk driving after *Spectator* Ball; 1 January 1960, climbing Trafalgar Square fountain.

Lady Mary Keen: Born 1940. Esteemed garden designer, writer and lecturer. Designed Glyndebourne Opera House new gardens and has completed many other large commissions. Recreation: gardening.

Linda Kelly: Writer and occasional journalist whose books include *The Young Romantics*, *Women of the French Revolution* and *Richard Brinsley Sheridan*. Currently writing a biography of the Irish poet, Tom Moore. Her husband, Lawrence Kelly, is also a writer, specializing in Russian subjects. They have three children and nine grandchildren and live in London and the Lake District.

Francis King CBE: Former international president of PEN and drama critic of the *Sunday Telegraph*. Has written twenty-eight novels, of which *The Nick of Time* (published by Arcadia Books) was listed for the Man Booker Prize 2003. Other fiction published by Arcadia includes *Prodigies* and *The Sunlight on the Garden* (2005). He was awarded a CBE for his services to literature.

Carl Kraag: Born in 1947 in Batavia (Jakarta), Indonesia. Is half Dutch and moved to Holland at the age of six. Studied art there and taught at the Academy in Amsterdam. In 1978 he moved to Italy where he runs – with his colleague, Walter Fabiani – a sensational antique shop in the medieval Via Battistero in Lucca. As you pass the window, you might well spot golden lacquered Burmese boxes, a Louis XV gilded console table, a pair of Louis XVI bedside cabinets from Naples and many treasures besides.

Lucinda Lambton: Lady Lucinda Worsthorne. Born 1943. One of our major television stars with silvery laugh and stunning looks. Honorary FRIBA since 1997. Many publications, including *Temples of Convenience*, *Chambers of Delight* and *Beastly Buildings*. Likes talking to dogs and watching pre-1960 movies. Married to the devastating Peregrine Worsthorne.

Kenneth Jay Lane: Before Kenneth Jay Lane came along it was socially unacceptable to wear costume jewellery. He revolutionized all that. He designed enamel bracelets, rings and collars of brilliant colours and studded with gems. The old prejudice was over. He did it single-handed. He has written on the subject in *Faking It*, appears on television regularly and is still startlingly handsome.

Tory Lawrence: Lady Oaksey. Born circa 1938. First half of life: competed on ponies and horses. Married young and ran Pinks Restaurant in Gloucestershire. Hunted for twenty-eight years while married to very nice husband. Since 1980 has led a less conventional life. Paints in England and abroad. Can often be seen in an old Mercedes with paints, canvasses and ill-assorted dogs.

Colonel W. G. A. Lawrie, MA, CEng, FICE, FIL, FRSA: He says of himself that 'without achieving any great distinction I believe I have made good use of what I learned at Cambridge and am now planning a new career at the age of ninety-one by setting up a school of bridge in Brazil.'

Timothy Leese: Garden designer. Studied decorative painting in Italy and worked in modern British pictures at Christie's. He has a nursery garden at Holkham Hall in Norfolk where all plants are propagated on site. Garden design takes centre stage.

Paddy Leigh Fermor: Sir Patrick Leigh Fermor DSO, OBE. Born 1915. Educated Kings College Canterbury. Traveller, writer, translator, hero. Winner of many literary awards. Wrote the Foreword to Miklos Banffy's *Transylvanian Trilogy* published by Arcadia.

Antony Little: Design director and cofounder of Osborne and Little, one of the leading names in British fabric and wallpaper designs. After studying in Flintshire School of Art, took a degree course at Kingston School of Art that awarded him the National Diploma in Design in 1963. Together with his partner, he has built up an international company with showrooms in London, New York, Chicago, Washington, Paris and Munich.

Roddy Llewellyn NCH, AI Hort: Garden designer, author, journalist, TV presenter, broadcaster, lecturer. His fascination for plants started when he was three and was given a tulip bulb. His books include: *Town Gardens*, *Beautiful Backyards*, *Water Gardens*, and *Elegance and Eccentricity*. Has received Silver Gilt at the Chelsea Flower Show and at the Hampton Court Flower Show. His achievements in the gardening world are too many to mention but, should you want advice, design or help of any kind with your garden, contact him immediately. Roddy Llewellyn, Old George House, Leafield, Witney, Oxfordshire OX29 9NP, Tel/Fax 00 44 (0) 1993 878700, Email: roddy.llewellyn@virgin.net

Rupert Loewenstein: Prince Rupert zu Loewenstein – Wertheim – Freudenberg. Educated St Christopher's Letchworth, Magdalen College, Oxford (MA). Financial advisor. Former merchant banker. C. St J., Knight of San Gennero, Knight Grand Cross of Honour and Devotion SMO Malta, Bailiff Grand Cross of Justice Constantinian Order of St George with collar, Knight of Justice Order of St Stephen. Recreations: music. Clubs: London – Beefsteak, Boodle's, Buck's, Portland, Pratt's, White's; NYC – The Brook, Regency.

John Lucas-Tooth: Sir John Lucas-Tooth Bt. Born in 1932. Educated at Eton where he won the Reynolds scholarship and went up to Balliol College, Oxford as an exhibitioner. First Class Honours in Physics. After taking a postgraduate degree in high-resolution optical spectroscopy, he worked with Professor Hall and, for seventeen years, designed, manufactured X-ray fluorescent spectrometers and sold them all over the world. He then worked in venture capital becoming a director of Lazard Investments Ltd. Now a director of Rupert Loewenstein Ltd and is chairman of several companies. Has Rolls Royce brain and is also secretary of the Beefsteak Club.

Candida Lycett Green: Born 1942, daughter of Sir John Betjeman CBE. Author, has edited her father's letters, written of the garden at Highgrove. Writes an inspired column 'Unwrecked England' for *The Oldie* magazine. Author of many other books, including *Over the Hills and Far Away*, a moving account of winning her battle with cancer and, more recently, *The Dangerous Edge of Things*, a village childhood.

Rupert Lycett Green: Astonishingly handsome and athletic. Bobsleighed for England in the Olympic team. Started Blades, the most elegant of men's tailors in the 1960s; his clothes are now to be found in the Victoria and Albert. Plays every known game: tennis, golf, and what you will.

Peter Mattingley: City and Guilds Advanced Craft painter and decorator. Well known for his skills, his wit and for the beauty of his wife and daughter.

Earl McGrath: Feral child in USA. Ran away from several foster parents. At one point lost a finger in a cement mixer. When the editor of this book lost two fingers in a car crash he rang her from New York 'as one amputee to another'. She found this extremely comforting. He is married to the marvellous Camilla and is a distinguished art dealer in New York.

Deborah MacMillan: Lady MacMillan. Painter. Born, Queensland 1944. Widow of Sir Kenneth MacMillan. Custodian of Sir Kenneth's choreography, which takes her spinning around the world. On a great many boards, all connected with the arts. Also renowned for her expertise in the breeding of Maltese Terriers.

George Melly: Jazz and blues singer of high renown. Appears frequently on radio and television; colourful dresser; brilliant raconteur and prolific journalist. He has written fifteen books, including *Hooked,* which tells of his overriding passion for fishing. His portrait by Maggi Hambling is a star exhibit in the National Portrait Gallery.

Christopher Miles: Educated at Winchester and the University Film School in Paris. Professor of Film and Television at the Royal College of Art, 1979-1983. Among his nine cinema feature films and supporting cinema features, he has been awarded Golden Globe and

Hollywood Oscar nominations, won the British Critics Circle and first prize at the Oberhausen and San Francisco film festivals. Won diplomas at Taormina, London, Belgrade, Cannes and San Diego festivals.

John Julius Norwich: Lord Norwich. Born 1929. Having spent twelve years in the Foreign Service, he left to write books. Has written histories of Norman Sicily, Venice and Byzantium; is now working on a history of the Mediterranean. For the past thirty-five years has produced an annual collection of bits and pieces which he calls *A Christmas Cracker*. Apart from that, likes to play the piano.

John Ogden: Born 1933. First a soldier, who helped to give away the British Empire, then an advertising man, who helped prop up commercial moves. Now a tyro novelist.

Milo Parmoor: Fourth Baron Parmour. Born June 1929, on the wagon since 1964. Likes food. Fancies newts. Did military service as lance corporal in Berlin and time in Harrods' sales-ledger department but failed to become an accountant. In the City for just under twenty years. Later, as owner of Quaritch, was in the antiquarian book trade for twenty-eight. Lives in London with weekends in Wiltshire.

David Plante: David Robert Plante. Born 1940, Providence, Rhode Island, USA. Paternal great grandmother a Blackfoot Native American. Dual nationality: American-British since 1995. Can say the word 'butterfly' in seven languages. Studied University of Louvain, Belgium and Boston College. Writer-in-residence at University of Tulsa, Oklahoma; L'Université de Quebec à Montreal; Gorky Institute of Literature, Moscow; King's College, Cambridge. Professor at Columbia University, New York since 1998. Awards: Henfield Fellow, University of East Anglia; Arts Council Grant; Guggenheim Fellowship; American Academy and Institute of Arts and Letters Award. Senior Member of King's College Cambridge, Fellow Royal Society of Literature. Publications: fiction includes *The Ghost of Henry James*, *The Family* and *The Catholic*: non-fiction includes *Difficult Women*. Lives in New York, London, Lucca and the Greek island of Paros.

Rex Pyke: Born 1940, itinerant filmmaker. In his own words: 'My father was lost at sea in February 1941, four months after my birth, without us ever meeting each other. For my first seven years, my mother worked as a nurse while I went to a series of boarding schools, staying on in the holidays. My mother married again (probably for my benefit) giving me an idyllic childhood in the perfect extended family. I have always worked in films and television, starting in a minor capacity on big films and now in a major capacity on small films. I edited five feature films, produced/directed films with Eric Clapton, Van Morrison, Joe Cocker etc. and television documentaries including *Dream Ticket*, *Lockerbie: A Night Remembered*, *Solway Harvester: Lost at Sea*, *In the Shadow of Foot and Mouth* and *Akenfield Revisited*. I produced and edited the film *Akenfield*.'

Paul Raben: Count Raben. Born circa 1950. Educated Winchester. Maintains that no portion of his life is respectable enough to mention. Tall, handsome, ineffably kind-hearted and friend of the editor of this book.

John Riddell: Sir John Riddell Bt. CVO. Born 1934. Thirteenth Baronet. Extra Equerry to HRH Prince of Wales since 1990. Lord-Lieutenant of Northumberland since 2000. Chairman of many distinguished companies. Wonderful host.

Nigel Ryan: CBE. Has just turned 75. I know because I went to a wonderful lunch party given to celebrate the event. He has a good head of hair. He is a some-time broadcaster and writer. Served as Reuters Correspondent in Rome, Baghdad, South Africa and the

Congo before transferring to television reporting. Editor of Independent Television News fron 1968 to 1977, then variously vice president of NBC in New York, director of programmes at Thames, and chairman of TV-am news. He translated novels from the French, including Maigret detective stories by Georges Simenon. Other publications include *A Hitch or Two in Afghanistan*, an account of the unsuccessful Soviet invasion in the early eighties and *The Scholar and the Gypsy, a search in Turkey for a Roman Fortress on the Eastern Frontier of the Holy Roman Empire*, co-authored with James Howard-Johnston, the Oxford historian. Recently – twenty years on – returned to Afghanistan on a charity walk to raise money for mine victims.

Jimmy Skinner: James Steuart Skinner. Born 1932. Educated Eton and Oxford. Economist and ecologist. Has lived in many African countries advising on economy. As well as serving on many other bodies, he is at present trustee of the Travel Foundation, New Economics Foundation and Elm Farm Research Centre. Director, Multimodal Finance Ltd, Bristol Electric Railbus Ltd. Associate, Forum for the Future. Loves Longhaired Dachshunds.

Jeffrey Smart: Born in Adelaide in 1921. Australia's foremost painter. Studied painting in Adelaide and Paris. Represented in the Metropolitan Museum of Art in New York and did the murals for the Opera House in Melbourne. He is crazy about Wagner and follows his operas around the world. Also crazy about Pugs – only has four at present. Lives in Tuscany.

Dan Somerville: Born in 1921, great-nephew of Edith Somerville. Worked for the British Council in Turkey, Jordan and Baghdad. Lives with his wife Celia in West Cork and Oxfordshire.

Lady Spooner: Wife of Sir James Spooner. Talented painter, expert bridge player and beloved ancestress.

Sir James Spooner: Born 1932. Educated Eton, Oxford RNVR. Director, John Swire and Sons 1970-2003. Chairman, NAAFI 1973-1987. Chairman, King's College, London 1986-1998. Director and trustee, Royal Opera House, Covent Garden 1986-1997. Chairman, British Telecom Pension Fund 1992-1998. Governor, St Andrew's Hos-pital Northampton 1970s to date. Governor, Royal Academy of Music.

John Stefanidis: World famous interior designer. Determined to be let off contributing to this book.

David Tang: Born in Hong Kong and educated there as well as in Cambridge, London and Peking, where he taught at Peking University. Worked briefly at Swire's, selling underwear before switching to a law firm and then worked for Algy Cluff on China oil exploration and African mining. Started his own business in 1990 and founded the China Clubs (Hong Kong, Peking, Singapore) and Shanghai Tang stores as well as becoming the exclusive distributor for all the brands of Havana cigars for Canada, Asia and Australia. Chairman of the Hong Kong Cancer Fund and the Hong Kong Down's Syndrome Association and trustee of the Royal Academy of Arts in London. On top of all this, he is a professional pianist.

Lady Anne Tree: Born 1927. Daughter of the tenth Duke of Devonshire. Widow of the painter, Michael Tree. Inspired gardener, scrabble player, needlewoman, dog-lover and artist.

Gilly Warrender: The Honourable Mrs Robin Warrender. Born 1931. Magistrate for twenty-five years, Bath and Swindon. Crazy about dogs, particularly strays. Has a passion for the origins of language and for clothes shopping.

Teresa Waugh: Lady Teresa Waugh. Daughter of the late Earl of Onslow. Brilliant novelist and translator from the French and the Italian. Her latest novel, *The House*, is a period piece describing post-war life in a cold and draughty stately home. She is Auberon Waugh's widow and lives in Somerset where she is at present researching the life of Arthur-Richard Dillon, the last and most splendid Archbishop of Narbonne who retired to London during the French Revolution. A superb cook.

Sophy Weatherall: Fisherwoman, gardener, provider. Ancestress, known as Super-Gran to many. Joint grandmother to eight with the editor of this book. Lives in Scotland.

Natalie Wheen: Born Shanghai 1947. Educated Downe House and London University. Broadcaster and writer. Has held many important posts in the world of musical broadcasting and is at present an incomparable and witty presenter for Classic FM. Hobbies: fishing, whisky, laughter and anarchy.

Martin Wilkinson: In his own words: 'I think the best description of me, apart from "old git", "idiot", "scarecrow" etc., which some might suggest – though not me, of course, I say modestly – might be something like "Farmer, author and songwriter".'

Vanessa Williams Ellis: Runs a service called 'Private Libraries' together with her companion in life, Richard Eeles. He is a qualified librarian, and she has experience from running a bookshop and is also madly efficient. They catalogue people's libraries, archives (papers, historical documents etc) and organize and maintain same. They produce printed catalogues or catalogues on CD. Email: richardeeles@hotmail.com. All this on top of running the farm.

Alice Windsor Clive: The Honourable Alice Windsor Clive, daughter of Lord Hylton of Ammerdown; was educated at Ascot, Oxford and the Courtauld Institute. She is a hard woman to hounds, knows every ordnance survey map by heart and is sister-in-law of the editor.

Richard Windsor Clive: The Honourable Richard Windsor Clive. Born in 1928, the son of the second Earl of Plymouth and fourteenth Baron Windsor. Educated Eton and Cambridge. He is a retired entrepreneur whose holding company acquired in the 1970s a major Dutch employment agency. Lives in the Exmoor National Park. He has been married at times, with seven children and stepchildren. At one stage he kept free-flying Blue and Yellow Macaws in the Brendons, until the fear they sometimes instilled and damage they caused to property and trees became unsustainable. He is a photographer, traveller and wit.

Sir Peregrine Worsthorne: Born 1923. Educated Stowe, Cambridge and Oxford. Writer. Exotically handsome and colourfully dressed. Former editor of the *Sunday Telegraph.* Is married to the wondrous Lucinda Lambton. His most recent book *In Defence of Aristocracy* was published by HarperCollins in 2004.

Victoria Zinovieff: A celebrated beauty. Born Victoria Heber Percy, daughter of another celebrated beauty: Jennifer Ross. Has worked as a therapist and is now a painter.

A percentage of *Late Youth* royalties benefits BTBS: THE BOOK TRADE CHARITY, helping colleagues in need. For further information, please contact: David Hicks or Jackie Bright at BTBS, The Foyle Centre, The Retreat, Kings Langley, Herts WD4 8LT, telephone 00 44 (0) 1923 263128